6/12/85

To Don
Best Wishes
Monty

Harry Lepp

# THE MONTANARI BOOK

# THE MONTANARI BOOK

## What the Other Child-care Books Won't Tell You

by A. J. MONTANARI

with ARTHUR HENLEY

STEIN and DAY/*Publishers*/New York

First published in 1971
Copyright © 1971 by Arthur Henley
Library of Congress Catalog Card No. 70-160346
All rights reserved
Printed in the United States of America
Stein and Day/*Publishers*/7 East 48 Street, New York, N.Y. 10017
ISBN 0-8128-1417-7

# Contents

    Introduction   7

    Preface to Parents   15

  I  Nose-Picking and Similar Habits   19

  II  Sex Play   29

  III  Stack-Blowing   39

  IV  Defecating and Other Natural Functions   49

  V  Physical Hangups   59

  VI  Lying, Cheating, and Stealing   69

  VII  Recklessness   81

  VIII  Sexual Peculiarities   93

  IX  Destroying   105

  X  Not Making It Intellectually   117

  XI  Tics and Fidgets   129

  XII  Being Fear-Ridden   139

  XIII  Sex Games with Adults   151

  XIV  Drawing into a Shell   163

    Postscript to Parents   175

    Index   185

# Introduction

These are the views of an audacious, nonconforming maverick who has devoted his life to helping parents cope with kids unable or unwilling to keep in step with society, their families, or themselves.

The problems dealt with here, although common to some degree in most normal childhoods, are generally considered unmentionable—and even insoluble—but not to Montanari.

First in his home, then at his clinical school and residential treatment center in Hialeah, Florida, he devised and practiced rehabilitative techniques that succeeded in retraining thousands of "impossible" children. He has even gone to jail on behalf of these kids to protect them against the indignation of neighbors who protested their presence in the community. But he was convinced that such reeducation could only take place in the child's natural habitat, in town, at home, wherever the child must live. Ultimately, his pioneering work won him recognition from such disparate observers as the late Senator Robert F. Kennedy, the American Psychiatric Association, and the distinguished dean of medical columnists, Dr. Walter C. Alvarez, emeritus consultant to the Mayo Clinic, who wrote: "My impression is that Mr. Montanari is one of the most useful and dedicated men in America."

His full name is Adelio Giuseppe Ambruano Pasquale Antonio Montanari, but the youngsters, parents, and professionals who know him best call him Monty. He is a handsome, chunky, powerfully built man in his early fifties who moves with the grace and the pugnacity of an athlete, talks in the blunt vernacular of a man in the street, and relates to children and parents alike with the gentleness of a man of the cloth.

He is casual rather than intense, accepting rather than demanding, and manipulating while appearing to be ingenuous. His unique abilities stem not from any formal training so much as from his own life experiences. From the emotional disturbance that lined his own childhood, Monty drew upon a deeply ingrained need to help troubled children in order to help himself. Out of this need came the drive that made his work not merely an occupation but a calling, a way of life, and that transformed his professional resources into mere extensions of himself. Having arrived at maturity without having shaken off the conditioning experiences that made him feel like a pariah, he developed a remarkable ability to "tune in" on other little pariahs, drawing upon his intuitive feelings and his academic training to make understanding them possible. You might say that he is like the alcoholic who, having cured himself, must go on to cure others in order to validate the cure.

I heard of him for the first time when I was researching a story about abandoned children for *McCall's* magazine. He was quoted in *Time* magazine as having criticized social workers for "setting up so many standards, to avoid the risk of failure, that most people can't qualify as adoptive parents, and so we have thousands of kids who stay in institutions because no one is allowed to take them." His contempt for procedure intrigued me. None of the established authorities whom I had interviewed had been so forthright. Here seemingly was a man who refused to sweep distasteful matters under the rug.

I telephoned him at Hialeah and found him even more candid. He spoke at length about his favorite subject—mixed-up kids and their distraught parents—and referred impatiently to the "endless array of tests, professional doubletalk, and time-consuming red tape" that seemed to impress everyone, but didn't help either the kids or their worried parents.

I visited him several times at Hialeah, worked alongside him, and shared with him both his frustrations and his insights about parent-child relationships. It was refreshing to discover that I had free access to any part of the clinical school and treatment center. In my experience as a reporter, I knew how difficult it was to obtain such access elsewhere, that troubled children always seemed to be hidden away from the view of reporters who wished to write about their plight. I always felt that such distrust of reporters chipped away at the credibility of the institutions charged with caring for such children. Monty put no prohibitions in my way.

"I don't want to shield my kids from society," he told me. "I want to expose them to it. That's part of my treatment, to bring these kids back into the community so they won't feel different and can learn to function among people."

He has a way of being to the point that used to shock me until I came to understand that his directness reflected his impatience with formalities that served to conceal problems rather than bring them out into the open. I saw him toss a seven-year-old high into the air, bringing squeals of laughter to the seemingly frozen child as he caught him in his arms, then say to me, "His mama has to peddle herself to keep this little fellow here. She's too proud to accept charity, I guess, or maybe she just feels responsible for his condition and she sells herself to get rid of her guilt feelings. But you know something? I have to admire a woman like that."

He doesn't attempt to impose his notions of morality, which are quite strict, upon others. He prefers to get to the heart of things. Moral questions are simply window dressing and could come later. Nor is he in a hurry to cram academics down the throats of kids with emotional problems. "If you've a child with an I.Q. of 140, but who spits in his mama's face," he once said to me, "what good is teaching him mathematics? He has to be taught to get along with his mama first."

The children in his charge range from age three to eighteen, and for all of them his credo is: "First reach them, then teach them." It was, and remains, his belief that kids at odds with society and with themselves must be motivated to change. He does not believe that parents should drive themselves to the point of despair because they feel responsible for their children's shortcomings. He knows what happens to a mother or father who goes from crisis to crisis, unable to resolve problems and therefore helpless to keep problems from snowballing. It is Monty's firm belief that if parents want to help their children, they must first help themselves, learn to tolerate stress, and relax their tensions, fears, and hatreds. By developing appropriate insights for themselves, they can manage to cope with a difficult child and teach the child himself to cope with them.

Whatever Monty learned did not come easily. He grew up in Winchendon, Massachusetts, the son of immigrant parents, and became the first in his community to be graduated from high school. While keeping up with his studies, he worked every day after school at the local cotton mill. He was the "mama's boy" that he describes in this book, tractable, attached to his mother, and taunted for it by his companions. "I had a terrible time as a child," he confessed to me. "I was a poor reader and couldn't concentrate on anything for long. I was often depressed. My parents were very strict and I guess I began rebelling at their rigidity."

However, some of this rebellion took healthy form. Monty defended smaller boys against the neighborhood bullies and, throughout his youth, helped others less capable than himself. Academically, he questioned everyone and everything. At Antioch College, he majored in psychology and social work but couldn't contend with the rigidities of his instruction. After three years, he quit college and joined the Army. But he kept going down the drain and flunked out of Officers' Candidate School. He was given a job teaching inept soldiers the art of riflery and, from this task, he mustered his own resources, finding satisfaction in teaching others. "I think the Army organized me," he told me, "by teaching me to follow through and building up my self-esteem." He worked his way up to sergeant, served overseas, was scarred in battle, and won the Bronze Star, the Purple Heart, and the Good Conduct Medal.

After being discharged, and following a number of odd jobs, Monty married and made his home in North Carolina where he worked at getting his degree in education at Western Carolina College. "That degree didn't mean a damn thing to me," he told me with a shrug, "but it seemed to mean a hell of a lot to the people I had to get along with."

He used the degree as a stepping-stone to becoming a teacher, then the principal, at a school for backward mountain children on the fringes of the Great Smokies. Most of these children, even those entering their teens, could barely read or write. Teaching them was an all-but-impossible task but it was a challenge that he enjoyed immensely. He succeeded in teaching these youngsters socially and academically, in that order, over the angry protests of their parents. He left to take a job in Miami, Florida, at a school for special children. "I learned there what *not* to do with troubled kids," he told me. "It became clear to me that I wanted to do things my own way. To do that, I had to have my own school."

On borrowed money, he bought a ramshackle old house for his family in Hialeah and begged the courts, the social agencies, and the local doctors to let him try to teach children they had found "hopeless" and had given up on. Word eventually got around that "if there's a kid nobody wants, send him to Monty." He began to rehabilitate these youngsters in his own home where they lived alongside his own son and daughter. It was very much a shoestring operation with many parents paying him on the barter system rather than in cash. But he worked with their children, who suffered all sorts of handicaps, on an around-the-clock basis, all the while wheeling and dealing his way to obtain financial support from local civic and service clubs. Success with these children led to respect by the professional people in the area who finally acknowledged that Monty possessed a rare ability to reach into the minds and hearts of troubled children, and to pass along his insights to their equally troubled parents.

It was 1952 when Monty established his school. Today, scattered within a radius of ten blocks are some twenty cottages housing more than three hundred children. There is nothing antiseptic about the setting. Each cottage looks like anybody's private house. There are spacious yards, bordered by palm trees, numerous classroom settings, workshops, and a diagnostic clinic. At Plantation Key, an hour and a half's drive away, is a separate sea camp; at Davie, near Fort Lauderdale, is a farm-and-ranch setting; and at Variety Children's Hospital is a special ward for youngsters requiring temporary hospitalization. A staff of two hundred fifty—including psychiatrists, psychologists, social workers, and houseparents—work under Monty's close direction and make use of all the community facilities, ranging from the public pool to the shops, theaters, and churches.

I have followed Monty's progress (and sometimes his lack of progress) for many years. Out of our meetings have come articles for leading magazines such as the *Saturday Evening Post*, several professional journals, and a book, *Demon in My View*, which deals in detail with Monty's life and work and is on the reading lists of psychology courses at many colleges and universities. Monty is a frequent speaker at university campuses, before professional organizations here and abroad, and on television. His disdain for academic degrees notwithstanding, he has been awarded an honorary LL.D. by John Marshall University.

The Montanari Residential Treatment Center, Clinical School and Hospital is the culmination of Monty's insistence on "doing his own thing," and doing it well. Dr. Povl W. Toussieng, a psychiatrist formerly with the Menninger Foundation and now Director of the Youth Counseling and Child Development Center associated with the University of Oklahoma School of Medicine, describes Monty as "a gifted person who does not pretend to be a psychiatrist but who uses a more intuitive approach than the average psychiatrist, and is helping more kids in one year than many of us manage to help in a decade."

But his most enduring compliments are paid to him by parents, and it is they who have supplied the questions he deals with in this book. Each chapter begins with a general discussion of the problem. The questions that follow deal with difficulties faced by real, individual children and their parents, even though some are phrased in a more general way than others. Monty's answers, though directed to the particular problems being raised, are intended to apply to the wide range of children who may have similar quirks or disturbances. These often embarrassing questions, if asked at all, are invariably answered with the catchall, "Go seek professional help." This is no answer. It is an evasion. For the first time, I believe that parents have at their disposal a book that doesn't evade ticklish questions. Monty stands up to the problems they represent as a parent might not be able to, but offers solutions that are within the parent's ability to carry out. He answers these questions directly, with concern not only for the child but also for the parents.

*Arthur Henley*

# Preface to Parents

I've written this book for parents who are willing to admit that kids aren't always "nice." Some children may have physical defects that bother them socially; others may be retarded or emotionally disturbed; most have *none* of these problems but still do some strange and puzzling things. There isn't a so-called "normal" kid who goes by the book all the time. Somewhere along the line of growing up, *every* child behaves in peculiar—even bizarre—fashion. Parents don't like to talk about this kind of thing, but many go to pieces because they don't know how to deal with their child.

If you're a parent, you know what I mean. You want to love your child but there are times when you can't show that love. Well, there's nothing wrong with that. You have feelings, too. But when you can't show love, you can show understanding. That's what love is all about, anyway, and every child knows it. And that's what this book is all about—understanding kids who aren't always lovable. They can't all go to psychiatrists to be made over.

Every time I hear or read about some expert or other recommending that when kids become too hard to handle, parents should "seek professional help," I have to wonder: Where do you find such help? Can you wait long enough to get it? Can you afford it?

I am all for professional help. I extend it myself at my treatment center. But I know from experience that such help is hard to find and very expensive. Treatment takes time. Then, too, some children may need residential care. That means going away (not being "put away") and good facilities are even harder to find and more expensive. Well, what does a parent do who can't find such help, or can't afford it? What's to be done if there's a long waiting list, maybe months, maybe a year or more, and help is urgently needed now?

You have to be realistic. You may have no alternative but to manage by yourself. The whole intent of this book is to show you how it is possible to manage the "impossible" child at home. It is my feeling that parents can do this if they know what they are doing and how much they are capable of doing. Some can do more than others, or in less time, so I've included a Postscript to Parents to help readers assess their parental goals and capabilities. Specific problem situations concerning various aspects of children's behavior are detailed in the Index in the back of the book.

I take the point of view that every parent is capable of doing something to make a child easier to live with. But first, it is important to relieve the parent's tensions and feelings of inadequacy. I don't believe there's a child alive who was ever helped by indicting the parents. If mama or daddy are blamed for the way their kids turn out, they will subconsciously take out their resentment on those kids, guaranteeing that the whole family will have more problems than ever. But if mama and daddy are helped to understand that they, too, are human, they will be able to manage their kids.

You see, it isn't words as much as attitudes that affect a child. Words are important—as I make clear throughout this book—but knowing how to use them is even more important. You can tell a child from now until doomsday: "Be careful" . . . "Stop playing with yourself" . . . "Study your lessons." Only the tractable child will listen. But the feeling you put into those words, the tone of your voice, your whole general attitude . . . these are what influence a child's behavior.

Unusually sensitive youngsters may experience day-to-day behavior problems that are more frequent and more intensive than the average child experiences. In the long run, this sensitivity may prove to be of great advantage in terms of future achievement. But sensitivity is hard to live with, hard on the child and hard on the parent. Parents sometimes hesitate to upset the delicate emotional balance of such a child. Fine. This is wise and considerate. But too much consideration can lead to self-sacrifice, and a self-sacrificing parent will ultimately also sacrifice his or her child.

What I'm trying to make clear is that parents must feel like somebodies in order to make their children feel like somebodies. Self-discipline is a necessity for every child who is to grow up emotionally healthy and self-sufficient. But it can't be instilled by a mother who goes around feeling no good because her child hasn't turned out the way she'd have liked, then blames herself, and then feels ashamed because sometimes she just can't stand the child.

I have a different philosophy. I say: some kids *are* harder to raise than others, and nobody knows why. Don't blame yourself. Give yourself the benefit of the doubt. Don't be afraid to use authority, but always temper it with understanding. Remember, there *are* times when a smack will do a child more good than a lecture, or depriving him of a privilege, or trying to reason with him. And there are times when parents have to join forces to outsmart a child whose cleverness at being difficult is upsetting the whole family. You have to try many approaches. You'll find that what works today may not work tomorrow, and vice versa. Just forget about the past and try to reconstruct the present by changing some part of the environment, some aspect of the parent-child relationship. I try to spell these things out in this book.

The questions here are the kinds I deal with every day in my work as a reeducator. I've used a lot of case material to make things clearer. I don't believe in using jargon, or in covering up "bad" thoughts or feelings with euphemisms. Polite language never cured anybody and very often serves to conceal the issue. The questions here *are* offensive in many instances. If we get uptight about them, we won't be able to resolve the problems they pose.

I've spent most of my life working with mixed-up kids of all ages, both sexes, and all sorts of hangups. Some have lived with me in my own home. I've worked closely with them and with their parents. Time after time, I learned that if I could make some little bulldozer behave for an hour, I could make him behave for two hours. And if I could make him behave for two hours, I could make him behave for a whole day. And if I could make him behave for a day, I could make him behave for a week, and so on. This has been my "formula" for bringing kids back into society, and all of them had problems like those I deal with in this book.

I know, as a parent as well as a reeducator, how you like to blame yourself for problems that affect your child. Stop blaming yourself; and come, let's see if we can't lick those problems before it's too late . . . before the schools reject your children because they're too hard to handle, before the doctors reject them because they're too hard to treat, and before you yourself reject them because they're too hard to love.

*Monty*

# I
## Nose-Picking and Similar Habits

Some bad habits are harder on the parent than on the child. A little girl who looks like a little ball of blubber because she gorges herself on food can be a source of shame to parents who place high value on good looks. But forever to be chastised and denied the extra helpings that she craves may be more upsetting to the child than being overweight. Less criticism from her parents and more from her friends might provide better motivation for eating less. On the other hand, the child who scrounges for everything from bits of broken glass to thumbtacks, then swallows them, is endangering himself and must be stopped. Parents have to distinguish between annoying habits that should be put up with and those that should be put down. To be able to do this, parents must learn to view habits in their proper perspective.

You don't need me to tell you how difficult it is to break a bad habit. If you've ever tried to give up smoking, drinking, or gambling, you know this. It's even more difficult to break someone else of a bad habit, especially a child. The longer the habit persists, the harder it will be to break. But the more intense parents become in dealing with the situation, the less likely it is that the child will listen. This is the vicious cycle parents find themselves in so many times. Feeling helpless, they become impatient and angry. This only serves to make a bad situation worse. There results a loss of reasonable communication between parent and child, even between the parents themselves, because they feel powerless, unable to control their kids. The home becomes a battleground for dominance. When things reach this point, the once awful habit seems of little consequence because now the whole family feels boxed in, and raw nerves begin to rub against one another.

Parents have to keep their sense of proportion, to weigh the need to do this or that, and above all to manage the situation in ways calculated to give them peace of mind. When anxiety, guilt, and anger displace peace of mind, the kids are likely to suffer more in the long run from continued parental annoyance than from the habits that led to that annoyance. In this chapter, we'll close in on some especially provocative habits that often lead to family turmoil and suggest a few remedies.

*How should you punish a child who picks his nose in class and whose teacher keeps writing notes about how disgusting it is?*

For God's sake, don't punish him. The boy has already been humiliated by having to bring home notes from his teacher, and there's a good possibility that the teacher has criticized him in front of the class. Don't shame him further. Talk to him. Tell him you don't care if he picks his nose from morning to night, but when he does it in front of other people, he looks pretty foolish. See that he carries a handkerchief in his pocket and tell him to do his picking in the handkerchief. You could remind him that if he digs too deep and cuts himself, he might get blood poisoning, and that would be very painful. Suggest that he doodle with a pencil when he feels tense instead of picking his nose. The most important thing is that you don't tell the child what his nose-picking is doing to *you*. The message to get across is what it's doing to *him*. It's making him look ridiculous to the girls in his class, and even to his boy friends, and it's making his teacher think badly of him. Then go to see the teacher. Explain that you were pleased to learn of her interest in your son but that you'd appreciate her not embarrassing him in class. And even if the nose-picking disgusts you as much as it does the teacher, remember that it's only a bad habit. It doesn't make him a slob or a delinquent or anything else except a little boy with a bad habit.

*Is it normal for a child to bite his toenails?*

It's normal for your child. That's why he does it. But this is a form of self-mutilation, like pulling out one's hair or picking at one's lip, and no parent likes a child to do this. Well, you won't help matters by slapping the child's hands or shrieking at him to stop. Try a more subtle approach. Fuss over his toenails. Get yourself a nice toenail clipper and clip your own toenails while the child is watching. Have your husband do the same thing. Chances are that the child will become intrigued enough to ask, "Can I try that?" Give him the clipper and show him how it works. He'll probably like playing with the gadget. Make him a present of it. I did this with a little boy and one day he told me proudly, "Hey, Monty, I don't bite my toenails anymore. I bite my fingernails!" Well, that's progress, isn't it? Now the thing to do is to encourage him to take pride in his fingernails. Show him how to use an emery board to keep his nails slick. If a girl has this habit, give her a manicure. Give the child a pack of chewing gum to keep his mouth too busy to bite his nails. Above all, don't make too much of nail-biting, even toenail-biting. This is the child's way of getting rid of anxieties and pent-up nervous energy. Provide some outlets for that energy —things to do, not just books to read or study. Many times, one habit will give way to another, and you just have to handle them one at a time without becoming overconcerned. Try to remember that whatever the habit, it bothers you more than it does him, and that isn't good for you. Find other things to occupy your attention in order to control your feelings, maybe even start biting your fingernails.

*What's wrong with an eight-year-old girl who insists on licking, smelling, and touching everything, even to the point of chewing other people's discarded gum and draining half-empty cocktail glasses after a party?*

Nothing is seriously wrong yet, but she could get sick if the original gum-chewer had a cold, or if she drinks too many cocktails. In any case, these habits should be discouraged promptly. The fastest way is to remove whatever sets them off. Get to the dirty cocktail glasses before the child can get to them, and don't ask her to help you clean up after a party. What is she doing up that late, anyway, hm? As for gum, no parent can follow a child around to see what she picks up. All you can do is tell her very plainly, no, she's not to chew somebody else's gum. And don't get all involved in giving reasons, just say no. I get the feeling, though, that because this little girl licks, smells, and touches everything, all these habits are part of her need to convince herself that she is alive and real and important. I'm sure she isn't very happy with herself. By sniffing or tasting what belonged to someone else, she is identifying with others whom she regards more highly than herself. It might be a good idea to be more attentive to her personal belongings: pick up her books and finger their pages lovingly; buy her an ice cream cone and ask for a lick; fuss over her clothes, her bedspread, her favorite possession, and admire these personal items. This tells her, in effect: "See, not only do I love you, I also love everything you have and would like to be like you if I could be your age again."

*Is there any way of getting kids to stop using gutter words like "fucking," "shitty," and "son of a bitch" in their conversation?*

Years ago we used to wash out their "dirty mouths" with soap. This gave them cleaner mouths, I suppose, but the words came out as dirty as ever—except that then they were used behind our backs. Well, this plainspoken language has become commonplace among today's "tell it like it is" generation. Good breeding has come to mean showing consideration for others rather than using polite language (often to conceal the lack of true consideration). Nevertheless, kids aren't being considerate when they deliberately offend their parents, who may not agree with their values. If you are such a parent, put down those kids without worrying about being mean or intolerant. Don't act offended, just plain annoyed. Tell such a child he's not to talk to you in those terms. Make it plain. Be as direct as saying, "When you decide to speak to me without using all that slang, I'll listen," then just walk away. If you handle it this way, without acting insulted or shocked, you'll get across the idea that this kind of language just isn't acceptable for no other reason than that you don't like it—period! I think you should remember, though, that these are only words. Many kids don't even know what they mean. They use them only to get a rise out of their parents so they can enjoy watching them squirm. Just stop squirming, but at the same time make it clear you don't approve.

*Shouldn't a six-year-old know better than to drool and dribble over his nice clean clothes every time he speaks or laughs?*

I guess he should, but maybe he can't avoid slobbering because of some speech defect. Have him examined by the family doctor or dentist, and also arrange for him to visit a speech therapist. If there is a defect, the only way to correct the problem is to have the defect removed. I raise this possibility because I've come upon similar situations many times. Now, on the other hand, this may be nothing more than a messy habit that the child doesn't want to give up. In that case, the more you fuss over his dribbling, the more he'll dribble to get your attention. Now, I know this won't please a mother who takes pride in her child's neatness, but what I would do is just stop making this boy wear such nice clean clothes. Let them be only clean and neat enough to look presentable, that's all. This isn't going to make him stop drooling over them, but it won't get mama feeling so upset when he does it because he won't be ruining his good clothes. When mama stops getting so upset, she won't make so much of the slobbering. When the child sees that nobody cares that much, he'll give up the habit because it's lost its value. Just put him in old, familiar, comfortable clothes for a while and see if this technique doesn't work for you. It's just possible that the child is demonstrating his dissatisfaction with nice clothes by slobbering over them.

*How do you put a stop to a youngster's embarrassing habit of zipping his fly up and down no matter who's around?*

First, try not to say, "Don't do that." It will call everybody's attention to the incident and cause you further embarrassment. He'll probably go on fiddling with his fly anyway and might create a scene if you insist he stop. Second, try very hard to conceal your embarrassment. Kids feel important when they see they have the power to make their parents feel uncomfortable. It's a good feeling, and like any habit that gives pleasure, it will be stepped up. Third, change the child's direction. You can do this if you haven't told him to stop and if you haven't revealed your embarrassment. Whatever you do now, you see, will not be connected with what the child is doing. He won't realize that you're trying to distract him. When you spot him toying with his zipper, just say casually, "Gee, honey, would you please turn off the light in the kitchen?" or "Go see if the dog's okay, I think I hear him scratching at the back door," or "Could you get me a glass of water?" Anything. Just give him something to do without making him—or your guests—aware that this is what you're doing. It comes out like a sudden thought, not a reprimand. Use variations on this technique when you see the child playing with his fly. Think ahead. Dream up ideas you can use when the occasions arise. After a while, he'll lose interest in the zipper. Now, should a guest ever mention this habit, I wouldn't think twice about telling such a meddler in a nice way to mind her own damn business. Just say, "I'll take care of it. Don't say anything to my son, please." A child shouldn't have to serve more than two masters: his mama and daddy.

*What discipline is appropriate for a young child who makes irreverent signs at church and shoots off his mouth blasphemously?*

Don't discipline him; outwit him. Such outrageous behavior could be the result of the family being *too* strict about churchgoing. My mother, for example, insisted on her kids' having a one hundred percent attendance at church. She wouldn't accept anything less, no matter what the reason. Well, that's being *too* rigid. That satisfies mama's needs, but not the kids', and they might rebel in outrageous ways. There's nothing wrong in saying to a reluctant child on an occasional Sunday, "Okay, so don't come to church today." But make churchgoing so enticing that he'll *want* to go and behave himself during the service. Make it worthwhile. After you tell him he can stay home, don't stop there. Say to him, "We aren't coming directly home after church is over, we're going on a picnic." You add an incentive, you see, in a sly way, not by telling him, "If you're a good boy, you'll get a treat." That's a bribe. You give him the right to refuse to attend church. *Then* you add, "We won't be home until about three, we're going to visit grandma." Now it's up to the child to backtrack if he wants to visit grandma with you. If he says he does, then you say matter-of-factly, "Okay, come to church with us and behave yourself." This way, you don't buy him off; you give him a surprise. And if he acts up in church, I know it will be hard for you to refrain from ordering him to cut it out. Try to control your irritation and just say, "Now, son, we're going home. I like you, but I won't tolerate this kind of behavior in church." Then get up quietly and take him home. On the following Sunday, say, "Do you want to come to church? If you do, you can't cuss there." Then use the "surprise" technique I mentioned earlier.

*When a ten-year-old thinks it funny to stick pins in her flesh, then suck at the blood, should she be hit?*

I wouldn't recommend hitting, but if it comes natural to

you and you swat spontaneously, don't feel badly about it. However, there are better ways to handle this. Try first to understand that this is not as unusual as you may think. A lot of kids pick up such habits around the age of ten. It becomes a contagious thing. One does it because everybody else is doing it. Now, you have to show some form of disapproval because it could be a dangerous habit. Explain to the girl that she could get blood poisoning or lockjaw. Tell her, "I'm going to have to put medicine on it." But instead of using mercurochrome, use iodine. I want to make clear that this is not a punitive technique. Your motive is not to punish, but to make an impression. You dab on the iodine, saying, "I know it burns, honey, but I can't help it. I don't want you to get sick." The pain isn't going to come as a great surprise to her. Most kids have a natural suspicion of medicines in general. As soon as she sees you reaching for that bottle of iodine, she might start yelling, "It's gonna hurt!" Don't deny it. And if she's still innocent about the ways of iodine, tell her in advance, "This is going to burn for a minute or two, so just grip my hand hard and yell all you want." By warning her beforehand, and by reassuring her while you dab on the iodine, you avoid making your action punitive. But the pain becomes a deterrent that should break the habit.

*Isn't age eight old enough for a child to stop wetting his bed and sometimes his pants?*

His pants, yes, but not necessarily his bed. Lots of kids go on wetting their beds because, for a variety of reasons, they feel anxious and want attention. If you satisfy this need in an understanding way and without becoming overanxious yourself, the bed-wetting and pants-wetting will stop. You don't say, "Goddammit, you pissed all over yourself again!" There's truth in the old saying that goes, more or less: "If a child knows you're excited and upset because of his behavior, he'll crap all over you." It's his way of getting your attention. But if you ignore him, that's another sign that you don't care. When you find his bed wet in the morning, the best thing is to treat the "accident" forthrightly, but kindly. Say to the child, "I don't know why you wet your bed, son, but I know that you're uncomfortable. Well, mommy and daddy are going to make you comfortable. One of us will wake you up during the night so you can go to the bathroom. Then your bed will be nice and dry and you'll feel good." Deal with the pants-wetting in a similar way. But remember, the child is embarrassed, so try to minimize his embarrassment. Just say, "Hey, you must be uncomfortable, son. Come on, let's change those pants before you get chafed." He might want to keep them on, probably to hide his embarrassment. Then you say to him, "Oh, let me help you change. Those wet old pants are going to get awfully smelly. That'll bother you and all the kids you play with. Come on, it'll only take a minute to change them." Stick with this technique. Unless there's a physical reason for his inability to control his bladder, he'll stop wetting. Pants-wetting leads to social ostracism, so give it priority.

*What can be done about a twelve-year-old girl who, despite a high I.Q., crawls on the floor when company comes?*

I.Q. has nothing to do with it. All it tells you is that this child isn't stupid, she knows what she's doing, and she must also know from everyone's attitude that her behavior is embarrassing. Well, fool her. Look upon her crawling around as a game she's playing. Get down on the floor and play the game with her. If a guest raises an eyebrow, don't apologize for the youngster's behavior—and yours—but just say nonchalantly, "We're playing a game." By handling the situation this way, you take the novelty out of the crawling. Kids become bored when the novelty wears off, or parents begin to cut in on their games. After a few minutes, I think you'll find that she becomes bored enough to quit the game. Now, if you don't feel comfortable doing this, or if it doesn't work, try another approach: rechannel her energy. Put her record player, radio, or favorite game on the floor to give her some excuse for crawling around. If one approach fails to work, I'm sure the other will. I'm assuming that, aside from this peculiarity, the youngster is well-adjusted. But if her crawling in front of company is only one symptom among many, you have to deal with each to alter her overall behavior. Also, you have to consider how long this has been going on, how often she does it, and what else is coupled with it. She may have a need to be babied more. In addition to dealing with each crawling situation as it arises, try being a little more demonstrative towards her at other times.

# II

# Sex Play

This is a confusing time for parents. On the one hand, their kids are being taught about sex in their schools, instead of in the streets, so that they'll know the difference between male and female and become more confident of their own sexual roles. On the other hand, society is encouraging a blurring of sex differences both socially and fashionwise. Then, to top everything off, pornography is becoming as respectable as apple pie. Well, it's no wonder that many parents are in a bind because they aren't sure whether to be lax or rigid in their attitudes about sex. When their kids indulge in sex play, they can't decide if they should feel alarmed or relieved. So, being good parents (and only good parents will take the trouble to read this book), they worry about what to think, what to say, and what to do.

I've had to help such parents, and their kids, cope with all kinds of erotic behavior ranging from the innocent to the brazen and the bizarre. Now, this is nothing new. As a child, I had my sex hangups, and I'm sure you had yours. Kids' instincts are no different today, but their inhibitions may be fewer. This leads many parents to wonder how their kids are going to grow up "straight," "normal," or "decent," with a genuine capacity to love and be loved in a world that seems far more mixed-up than that of your generation and mine.

Today's kids need to adapt to different standards and to form new personal values. Nevertheless, despite the current frankness about sex, some basic notions concerning propriety and healthy sexuality remain as valid as ever. At one time, for example, nobody dared talk about incest; today it's discussed more openly but its practice is still taboo. Homosexuality has its enthusiasts but heterosexuality is still the way to go. Because we have become more progressive, we can talk about sexual deviation with less shame and with more understanding, but it doesn't mean we should endorse it.

With all our sexual progressiveness, however, parents continue to fret when they find their child and the kid next door playing doctor together. Well, sometimes they should fret, but other times they shouldn't. All erotic games are not alike, nor do they affect all children, or all ages, in the same way. It is natural for some kids to be more sexually precocious than others; it doesn't make them "bad."

I would caution parents to think twice before characterizing any child as a deviate, no matter what sort of sex play is witnessed or reported. But parents do have to know how to detect and put a halt to the kinds of sexual behavior that can mess up a child's life. The important business of separating the harmless from the harmful is the subject of this chapter.

*What do you do with a ten-year-old girl who hides in the bushes with boys and giggles while she lets them smell her panties?*

You don't do anything if that's all she does and she doesn't do it often. Just keep an eye on her, that's all. If there's a certain boy who is encouraging her to do this, you might do something about discouraging him from seeing her. But this little girl isn't abnormal. What she is doing isn't unusual. To my knowledge, nobody ever did a study on how many little boys like to smell little girls' drawers, but I'll bet the results of such a study would be surprising. I know I did such things as a little boy; so did my friends and most of the kids I've known in my lifetime. Naturally, sex play of this nature is likely to upset parents. But in my judgment, it's nothing to worry about unless the child finds nothing else to giggle about. I'd make an issue of it only if this kind of play has become an obsession with her. Then what I'd so is to distract her, keep her busy, manipulate her time so that she's too preoccupied to bother getting involved with boys. You may have to redecorate her room or spend more time with her or assign her more responsibilities, but whatever you do, do it casually and give her tasks that interest her. Don't give her opportunities to be alone with boys whose chief interest is the exchange of such intimacies. But don't make a fuss about things. This is usually just a phase in growing up, so don't read any more into it than that. Just take sensible precautions to see that she gets through this phase without being overstimulated.

*If your fourth-grader tells you he compared penises with a classmate and confides proudly, "Mine's bigger!" how do you answer him?*

You just nod pleasantly, say "That's nice," and stop worrying that you're raising a potential homosexual. It is very common for small boys to compare penises. Sometimes they're obvious about it ("You show me yours and I'll show you mine!"). But most times they just steal glances at one another when they're undressing at the school gym or when they're skinny-dipping at the pool. Some teenagers, and even grown men, never stop sizing themselves up in comparison with other males, checking out everything from the hair on their chests and genitals to the length and design of their equipment. Girls and women compare busts and pubic hair in the same way. There's nothing to be alarmed about. In fact, a parent should feel relieved when a child confides such information; it indicates good, healthy communication between child and parent. Actually, all that these kids are doing is expressing curiosity about their bodies and reaffirming their sexuality. Sooner or later, of course, a boy will discover that other boys have larger penises, and a girl will discover that other girls have superior chest development. So what? These differences don't diminish their sexuality. But when a child confides such information, the parent has a fine opportunity to mention that boys are boys, no matter what size their penises, and girls are girls, no matter how developed their busts.

*What should you say to a son and daughter—he's seven, she's six—whom you suspect of sex play in their room?*

If you only suspect them, you shouldn't say anything, but you should definitely do something. And the first thing you had better do is get them separate rooms. If this isn't possible, build a partition. These kids need privacy. Separate rooms will deprive them of opportunities to mess around together. But these children are still young enough to be quite innocent of anything to be concerned about. I mean, what kind of sex play do you suspect? That they were looking at each other's nakedness? That they were ogling their sexual differences, his maleness and her femaleness? I know it's natural for a mother to be startled at seeing her two kids—especially of different sexes—romping together in the nude, but maybe that's all they had on their minds: a nude romp together. Hm? I'd guess that they were exploring their sexual differences and were pretty surprised to find that they were different. And maybe they were even poking at each other with their fingers, touching. Well, it's only natural curiosity that's motivating them, but it has to be discouraged because these are brother and sister, even though they're unaware that what they're doing is "wrong." But you can't become panicky and yell, "Stop that!" That will terrify the children and they're likely to feel that all sexual curiosity is "wrong." Just keep them separated, that's all. As they grow older, they may have incestual fantasies and masturbate. There's nothing wrong with that as long as they do it privately. Give them that privacy now.

*Is a twelve-year-old boy of good character a pervert because he was pulled out of line by his school guidance counselor for "molesting" the girl in front of him (a girl he'd grown up with) by tugging playfully at her skirt?*

No, but I think the guidance counselor probably is. It's damned unfortunate that many people who are supposed to educate youngsters socially are so uptight that they have forgotten the meaning of innocence. "Molesting" is a harsh word. Was the boy leering, or was he smiling? Did he goose the girl or take other liberties, or did he simply give her skirt a playful tug? Come now, if he really wanted to molest her, he sure as hell wouldn't have chosen to do so in the school hall in front of everybody! Besides, she is a girl he's known all his life, and their parents must know one another well. Only a damned fool or a very sick youngster would try to tangle with a girl who could report him to her folks. This is a boy of good character, and how sad it is that this fine, innocent child should become the victim of this dirty-minded school official. Unfortunately, because there are a few troublemakers in most schools, some guidance people are so scared, or so incompetent, or so prurient, that they see the worst in any child who doesn't make himself invisible. It's the counselor, not the child, who needs guidance. The parents should stand by their son, make light of the situation, and quietly pay a visit to the school to make absolutely sure that no blemish has been put on the boy's record that will follow him around the rest of his life.

*When a big, well-developed girl likes to wrestle with other girls, is she being sexually stimulated by this kind of play?*

I would think so. All physical-contact games have some sexual content. And a girl who's starting to blossom into womanhood is certainly receptive to sexual stimulation. I don't think these wrestling matches are healthy for her. If she wrestled with boys, I'd suspect that the two were using the game as an outlet for their natural heterosexual urgings. It's a normal outlet and doesn't generally lead to intercourse. In fact, it usually is a substitute for more intimate sexual expression. But here we have a situation of sex play—wrestling—between girls. When it occurs frequently, there is reason to be concerned. It could set up a homosexual pattern. I wonder—who initiated these games? Is this girl being seduced, or is she the seductress? Is this girl unpopular with boys, or has she been warned about sex over the years so that she just doesn't trust boys? A perceptive parent will get some insight into this youngster's feelings by answering these questions in all honesty. At this point, the wisest thing a parent can do is to interrupt these games as casually as possible. When the family is gathered around the dinner table, introduce sex into the conversation by mentioning some item in the newspaper about women's lib, or unisex clothes, or a controversial movie on a homosexual theme. Why? To bring the girl into the conversation and sound out her feelings. This can break the silence that prevents an exchange of opinion between children and parents. It gives the parents a wedge to influence the kids without being obvious and without the need to deliver a lecture.

*When your well-mannered ten-year-old shames you by taking snapshots of his genitals to show off to girls, what else can you do except take away his camera?*

Some psychiatrists would say that taking away his camera is like taking away his genitals. Maybe so. Anyway, taking away the camera isn't a solution. The boy could draw pictures of his genitals and keep showing off. I get a feeling that the camera is the key to getting this "well-mannered" ten-year-old back on the right track socially. He's probably a pretty good little photographer. I'll bet he's taken lots of good pictures but maybe no one in the family has really paid much attention to them—until now. So he thinks to himself, "Damn it, nobody looks at my pictures of flowers or anything else, so I'll use my camera on something that'll make them take notice!" It's the same way some advertisers think when they use sensationalism to attract attention. If I were this boy's daddy, I'd say, "Hey, son, I didn't know you were so talented. Let's see your other pictures." I'd show my appreciation of those other pictures and encourage him to take more like them. I might even help the boy develop and print his films. I think there's also the real possibility that this youngster has become very conscious that he is maturing. He's proud of growing up and wants to be told, "Say, you're getting to be quite a man!" I'd make him feel more grown-up and might even say, "You don't have to take pictures like this to let people know you're a big boy." I wonder, too, if the girls didn't do something to encourage such photography, a kind of subtle seduction. Check around. In any case, don't jump on your boy. Just use the techniques I suggested to put a stop to his exhibitionism.

*It's an awful shock when your twelve-year-old daughter's handbag opens accidentally, condoms spill out, and she admits she's had intercourse! How should a parent deal with this?*

Don't become so alarmed. This may surprise you, but just because this girl admits she had intercourse doesn't mean it's so. Lots of young boys carry condoms in their pockets for a long time before they ever get a chance to use them. I did it myself, to be a big shot among my friends, to be in with the crowd, many of whom were older than me. You can't always deal with isolated incidents. You have to consider the whole personality of the child. I imagine you know who your daughter's boyfriends are. If they're her age, don't get too excited, she's probably just bragging. All right, now suppose that she really means it, that she has been having sex. Well, you can't give her license. I don't believe in saying, "Okay, honey, I'm glad that at least you're using protection." This is why I don't approve of doctors' writing prescriptions for birth-control pills right off the bat. If you're pretty sure that she has been having sex, you have to take parental liberties and say no to such behavior. She is too young for this. Don't give her a bawling out because that won't help. You have to establish communication, trust—something that obviously hasn't taken place or else she wouldn't be so sneaky. She knows you disapprove. Now you have to explain why. Don't talk about morality. Talk about the dangers of venereal disease and out-of-wedlock pregnancies. She'll say, "That's why I make the boy use condoms." You say, "Fine, they usually give protection, but sometimes they break." Then, having initiated a conversation in this way, you'll find her more receptive to arguments about how promiscuity will mess up her reputation, and her life.

*If you happen to see your friend's son expose himself to your daughter (she's in the fourth grade), how do you handle the situation?*

Distract your daughter's attention at once. Call out, "Hey, sweetie, I've been looking all over for you. I want you to go shopping with me." Use any excuse to get her away. What you do next depends on the effect of the incident upon the girl. Does she mention it? Does she express shame, indignation, disgust? Does she tell you that she felt embarrassed and was just about to walk away when you called to her, or is she still too innocent to feel embarrassed? What you say to her depends on what she tells you, if she tells you anything at all. I wouldn't make much of the matter if she indicated that she was about to turn away abruptly and leave. That's healthy. I'd just shrug my shoulders and say, "That boy was making a fool of himself. I'm glad you realize that." But if I got the impression that she was staring, spellbound, getting pleasure out of the fool's exhibitionism, I'd be concerned that she hadn't been sufficiently informed about sex differences. That kind of curiosity should have been satisfied before kindergarten age. Without making too much reference to the incident, I'd begin educating her sexually in order to blunt such curiosity. This is the time, long past due, for mama and daughter to have a heart-to-heart talk about the difference between the sexes. Now, if she doesn't talk about the incident, then I'd bring it up myself; I wouldn't bury it as if nothing had happened. Something has happened, and she's uptight about it. I'd just say, "That boy acted pretty foolishly, don't you think?" This would give her a chance to explain her own feelings and give me a chance to explain why such exhibitionism isn't socially acceptable. You see, it's not what the boy does, but what the girl does, that would concern me. But I'd tell the boy's mama about it.

*Should you punish a girl who is entering junior high school but who looks more mature than her age and insists on wearing very short skirts, no bra, and even see-through blouses?*

I prefer taking parental license to dealing out punishment. It may not do any good, but you don't have any alternatives. If this girl insists on presenting herself so seductively now, she is well on her way to behaving like this forever. All you can do now is apply parental license, say no, firmly and adamantly, without giving an inch if she raises hell. You have to step down hard. That's your prerogative, and you should exercise it. Apparently, she is assuming that she can manipulate you and do what she wants. Don't threaten her, don't scream at her, don't call her names. But very firmly say to her, "When you leave this house, you leave the way I want you to leave, and dressed the way I expect you to dress!" Now, I admit that putting your foot down this way is a calculated risk. You might very well create a different person. She could develop a great deal of resentment and act out such feelings in more subtle, more secretive ways. In other words, by facing up to her, you could drive her underground. But this is a risk you have to take. It should be the school's prerogative to send her home if she comes in wearing a see-through blouse. In the long run, however, it's up to the parents to reshape her attitudes. Whether she goes to school or to a party, parents have to say "No" to social attitudes that work against the child's best interests. You can't be like the mama whom daddy tells, "Leave her alone, don't upset yourself." You are upset. Be reasonable, but don't be afraid to say "No." On the other hand, if it's more your style, you might have to say, "Dress as you wish, but not with my blessing." It's still better than punishment or doing nothing.

*If you catch your eight-year-old with his hands up the skirt of the little girl next door (she's four), what do you do?*

You take drastic action. This is unhealthy for everyone concerned—your son, the little girl, and both families. You take the boy aside at once and just say simply, "That's not right. Don't do that again." No explanations, only a directive. This isn't sniffing panties, it isn't even playing doctor. It is a situation that is potentially explosive emotionally and socially; it could even lead to the boy's being singled out for rejection and humiliation by the community if word about his behavior gets around. If this is the first time he's done this, consider yourself—and the child—lucky that you happened to catch him at it. If you find that your son has taken similar liberties before, be glad that you finally discovered what's been happening. As young as the boy is, keep in mind that the little girl is even younger. When he puts his hands up her skirt, he is taking advantage of her tender age and her innocence. But there is nothing innocent about his behavior, or he wouldn't be adventuring so deviously. There would be less need for concern if this young fellow stripped down with a girl his age with each peering at the other out of mutual curiosity. Nothing of the sort is going on here. It is a pretty clear case of a small boy exploiting a still smaller girl because she is a less threatening sex object than an older girl would be. You can't permit him to do this. In addition to taking a strong stand against such behavior, you should restrict the opportunities for this boy to be alone with little girls. Your disapproval may be all that's necessary to prevent similar sex play in the future. But you'll have to accompany such disapproval with some straight-from-the-shoulder talk about sex to remove the *need* for such devious gratification.

# III

## Stack-Blowing

When a child's temper flares up into a full-fledged tantrum, it's often enough to make a mother wish she'd never given birth. The unreasonable anger can be frightening. And since any show of temper is a show of potential violence, it tends to be responded to just as violently with shrieks, beatings, or door slams.

Such passionate feelings are evidence that parents, too, are human, and not that they're rotten parents. Of course, it's far from the best way to handle a child who's blown his stack. Nor is it a time to wonder about the how and why of such behavior. It is a time only to calm the child as quickly as possible. This requires a calm parent, and the achievement of such calm requires some insight into the way parents feel as well as into the way children feel.

In my experience, both as a father and as a professional person, I have yet to come upon a child who is not frustrated now and then in some way or other. Now, not all frustrated children blow their stacks. Some take their frustration out on themselves, hurting themselves or withdrawing from society, and these outlets can be worse than letting go. Nor do all kids who do let go reach the same heights of fury. Each child deals with the problem in his or her own way. No one can say for sure if this comes about as a result of the child's constitutional endowment or as a customary behavior pattern conditioned by the child's upbringing. So there's no reason to believe that the child who goes wild at the slightest provocation is the product of parents who are ogres.

I think parents simply have to expect a certain amount of

disrespect, intolerance, and tantrums as the penalty for parenthood. This doesn't mean their child loves them less or that they've made a botch of being good parents. It only means that this is par for the course. No one is infallible, and kids are unpredictable. Once a parent recognizes these facts, the mystique goes out of parenthood and good sense prevails.

Good sense means knowing when to punish and when to cop out, when to speak up and when to be silent, when to advance and when to retreat. Kids who go off the deep end have a way of destroying parents' self-esteem. This is the beginning of family disaster. Parents must keep up their self-esteem in order to deal with children who aren't sure of their own, as this chapter attempts to make clear.

*How do you cure a perfectionist? It's unbearable!*

I know it's unbearable, but you don't "cure" a perfectionist. You just have to reeducate him to put up with mistakes. I had a six-year-old boy living with me who was a perfectionist. He had a one-track mind. Everything he did had to be just right. He couldn't tolerate mistakes. If he made an error in his lessons, he'd tear up his paper and blow his top. I watched him do this time after time. One day, I took him aside after such an episode and after he'd cooled down. Picking up a pencil, I said, "George, why do you think they put erasers on pencils? Do you know why?" Well, he just looked at me and didn't answer, so I answered my own question. "To correct mistakes, that's why," I told him. "Everybody makes mistakes, you see. That's why they invented the eraser." I wrote my name on a piece of paper, deliberately misspelling it, then rubbed it out with the eraser. Then I corrected the spelling. Then I did the same with his name, misspelling it, erasing it, and correcting it. I made it seem like fun. I stressed the fun, not the fact that erasing saves time and effort. And I didn't lecture George. I said what I had to say once, then stopped. It took a while but eventually he came around and began to use his eraser. In a way, I think this was George's first real step to overcoming his fears. When a child isn't afraid, you see, he isn't afraid to make mistakes. He knows he'll be loved, imperfections and all.

*Should a boy who goes into frequent rages and bites his father be bitten back to teach him a lesson?*

Well, it may give the boy's daddy some satisfaction, but I don't think it's going to do the boy any good. I just don't believe a parent should stoop to the child's level and imitate the child's behavior. I knew a hot-tempered little girl who'd get so mad she'd tear up the new clothes I'd bought for her. Well, I didn't shove those clothes down her throat and make her eat them. I felt like doing it, I'll tell you, but I knew that wouldn't help the child. But I didn't condone her behavior, either, by patting her on the head and saying, "There, there, be a good little girl." She couldn't be a good little girl, you see. She was too sensitive to respond to frustration like a good little girl. If I had tried to make her behave like one, it would be like telling a blind child, "If you stumble over the coffee table, I'll beat the hell out of you." This was a child who couldn't help blowing her stack. Same as the boy who bit his daddy. These are kids who haven't yet learned to control their impulses when they feel cornered. But you don't teach them a lesson by behaving just as foolishly. What do you do? Well, you lick your wounds privately—after you give the child a quick whack on his bottom to let him know—and feel—that you won't put up with his biting. I don't hold for corporal punishment, but in cases like this it's the most effective way to get across the message: Control yourself. A single swat at the moment of misbehavior, just one quick good swat, not in anger, not in hate, just plain calculated and promptly administered, can educate the child to learn self-control.

*Why does one child throw a fit every time her mother wants to go out when none of her brothers or sisters act this way?*

I'm not sure I know why, but I do know that each child is

unique even within the same family. Some are very jealous of their siblings. I heard one little boy complain to his mother, "You play mommy to them instead of me." He wanted her to himself, that's why. In fact, the youngster was so unsure of his parents' love that he accused his daddy of getting up early and leaving home before he, the child, was awake, just to avoid kissing him goodbye. He manipulated his mama in all kinds of ways to keep her home. He played sick; he threw tantrums; he even held her against the wall to prevent her from leaving. Well, a mother can't allow herself to be manipulated by her child. The more she gives in, the more dependent that child will become. She'll be encouraging such dependency without realizing it. Is it possible that the little girl in the question above is afraid to be alone? Then see that someone remains with her until she learns to overcome such fears. It seems more likely that she doesn't feel as sure of your love as do her brothers and sisters. Frankly, is she less fun to be with than the other kids so that unconsciously you pay her less attention? Whatever the reason, here's a technique I've seen succeed for parents in similar difficulties. When you wish to go out, remind her that you are also leaving the other children. Most importantly, tell her you will be home at such-and-such a time—and be damned sure to be home by that time! All I'm suggesting is that you deliberately make a promise and keep it. Do that several times and she'll begin to feel surer of your love and of your return. It may not mean much to you to be five or ten minutes late, but that child will be watching the clock. Don't disappoint her.

*How do you handle a six-year-old who bangs her head violently against anything—a table, a chair, even the pavement—when she can't have a treat?*

First you must protect the child from hurting herself. You can't let her go on banging her head that way. Pick her up, or get down on the floor with her, and hold her close to you. Try to soothe her. Don't say anything, just "Shhhhhh. . . ." She'll probably scream, cry, and fight back at you. Let her, but keep holding her close. Use all your strength because your strength will give her strength. At first she'll use it to battle you, but you're stronger so eventually she'll tire out. Ultimately, that strength will transfer itself to her emotions and she will feel protected by your arms instead of feeling stifled. When she's simmered down, you can start to talk to her, softly, without anger or recrimination. Say to her, "Honey, if you want that candy so bad, I'll get it for you when I can. But if I don't think you should have it right away, you just have to be patient until I'm ready to get it for you. And I'm not going to get it for you if you go on hurting yourself by acting up this way. Because then you'll be so unhappy you won't be able to enjoy eating your candy." Let her sulk for a while, then tell her since she's been such a good girl, you're going to get her the candy right after she's had her lunch (or dinner). In other words, teach her to understand that her good behavior will be rewarded within a reasonable time. This will teach her the value of acceptable behavior and the ability to endure frustration.

*What can be done with a child who for no reason goes berserk, literally terrifying the entire family?*

This is a very angry child, and you can be sure he does feel he has reason to be so angry. I'm sure his behavior is way out of proportion to whatever provocation he might feel, but kids don't think the way grown-ups do, especially kids with a low boiling point. I've had lots of kids say to me, "Monty, when I get mad, you believe I have a reason, but most people don't think I have." As a parent, you have to keep this in mind when dealing with the child. Remember, too, that a kid who can intimidate a whole family knows he can get away with it because everyone's afraid of him. It is a frightening display. But try to think of his bad temper as a kind of blemish on his personality, the way a wart would be a blemish on his body. Now, you wouldn't be afraid of a child who had a wart, would you?

All right, he's got a wart that erupts into some violent shenanigans: cussing, maybe smashing things, and screaming like fury. But there's more swagger and threat in his manner than there is actual violence. Bear this in mind and stop being afraid. Assume that no one is going to be attacked physically, as I'm sure they won't be—unless this child is pushed to the breaking point. Let him rave, but you be quiet. Try to go about your business even if he screams louder. Above all, don't try to cut him down with comments like, "Stop acting like a jackass!" He'll only feel belittled and will be more infuriated. Eventually he'll calm down. Put your arm around him and give him a hug. He might say, "I was mad." Just nod and reply, "When you feel like it, will you tell me why?" Give him time. He'll tell you. This approach will bring the two of you closer and help him drain off some of his aggression.

*When should a child be locked in the bathroom as punishment or tied to a bedpost to keep him from going berserk?*

Never! You never lock a child in a room by himself and you never tie him down. I've spent lots of time with little hellraisers so I know what a parent must endure with such children. But locking them up or tying them down is only going to make things worse for everybody. Even if your child is hurting himself, please don't tie him to the bedpost or anything else. Sit with him, hold him, soothe him until he's able to control himself. Remove any irritants that might have triggered the tantrums. If he wants to smash the television set because he doesn't like the program, turn off the set. If that's not enough, move the set out of the room. As for locking him in the bathroom as punishment, that's for the birds. The worst thing a parent—or a professional—can do is put a child in isolation. That's the supreme rejection. It's a terrifying experience. I never believed in so-called "quiet rooms." It's easy to say, "Okay, you're a bad boy, I'm going to lock you in the bathroom." But this is one easy route you can't take. What you can do is say,

"You're a bad boy. Go to your room. Then when you feel like behaving like a human being, come on out. We want you out here." That's a different thing, you see. It's the child's room and you're sending him there, you're not locking him up. You're telling him, "Because your behavior is intolerable, we must remove you from the company of your family, or your peers. But the minute you decide you want to be one of us, come on out. We want you." It's a reasonable way of letting the child know that his behavior must be acceptable—appropriate to whatever the custom is at your home. You don't tell him to stay in his room "for an hour" or "until I tell you to come out," but "whenever you're ready."

*How do you console a child who hates one parent and raises a tremendous fuss demanding that the parents get a divorce?*

The first thing I'm prompted to say is that this is none of the child's business. You must make that emphatic and tell the child, "This is not your concern. You cannot dictate to your mama and daddy. If we decide to divorce, then we'll do it. But we must make that decision, not you." All right, let's assume you've been fighting together and, rightly or wrongly, the child has gotten the impression that you and your spouse can't get along, you're miserable living together, and so on and so on. Maybe so, but it's not for the child to make the decision. Lots of couples fight constantly but, strangely enough, this is the very thing that keeps them together. Somebody once called these "marriages based on mutual hostility." In their own strange way, I suppose these might be characterized as good marriages—not because they're happy, but because there's something in the relationship that satisfies the needs of both partners. Now, this is too much for a child to understand. He's going to take sides, favor one parent over another. This is understandable, and a child who must learn to live in this battleground does need consolation. So you say to the youngster, "Yes, mama and daddy are having trouble. We do fight sometimes. But we want to stay together because we love each other and because both of us love you." In other words, you take the child into your confidence to a point, to ease his anxieties. But you mustn't let the child control your destiny, or he'll control you forever at high cost to his own mental health.

*How do you answer a hot-tempered child who throws back in your face, "You scream, why can't I!"?*

You turn the tables on the child. "You're right," you tell him, "I do scream. Will you help me stop?" Instead of your trying to correct the youngster, give him the responsibility of trying to correct you. You're in a situation where this kind of honesty will produce results where chastisement will not. Level. Say to your child, "Screaming is one of my weaknesses. But even your mama is entitled to have some weaknesses. I'm human, too, you see. But I wish I didn't have this particular weakness. So how about you helping me the same way I try to help you when you do things that I don't like?" You're giving the child an opportunity to put a stop to something he doesn't like: your screaming. I think you'll find he'll take the challenge to help you because he's the top banana, he's getting a chance to call the shots. This is fine. In trying to help you, he's going to help himself stop screaming and showing temper. Whenever a child tells me "You swear, why can't I?" "You burp, why can't I?" or "You do this or that, why can't I?" my answer is always, "Fine, I admit it. I want to stop but I can't. Let's work something out where you will help me stop." Kids are stunned by such an admission of weakness and very flattered that mama or daddy is asking for *their* help. This technique also brings with it an extra dividend. By working together with your child this way, you'll find yourself developing a new closeness to the child that will help you to resolve other problems that eluded you before.

*Should you ignore an angry child who tells you to drop dead?*

You shouldn't ignore whatever a child does. You should consider all the things you might do and then make a decision. One thing you might do is overlook the remark. That's not the same as ignoring it. To ignore means to cast aside without making a decision. Now, if this is a child who has a lot of emotional problems, overlooking his impudence may be the wisest decision if you can do it comfortably. It is sometimes better to deal with a highly emotional youngster this way than to try to cut him down to size. Cutting him down may produce stronger remarks than "drop dead," and may lead to acting-out behavior that is far worse. He might smash windows, break up the furniture or run away. If you are able to shrug off the remark, though, the words will lose their potency to the child and he'll stop using them. On the other hand, this might simply be a fresh kid, or at least a kid who's being fresh at this time. That's a very different thing. You can't afford to lose respect. Do whatever comes naturally. He's earned the right to be slapped, or receive a verbal reprimand, or a stern look of disapproval. The best response would be to tell him firmly, "Don't ever speak to me that way again!" and to walk away from him, letting him stew. Just don't start screaming and making a Federal case out of the remark. Because he tells you to drop dead doesn't mean you're going to. It's a bratty remark, that's all. Just consider the sort of child this one is generally before deciding how to react.

*Are drugs the best way to quiet a rambunctious child who blows his stack at the least provocation?*

Drugs should be a last resort, to be used only when every other technique has failed, and then only long enough to make the child amenable to other techniques. I don't believe in committing chemical warfare on a child. Patience, understanding, counseling . . . everything else comes first. You have to remember, too, that children just aren't alike. Some *have* to be hyperactive and a bit rambunctious, at least to a degree. It's part of that child's personality. He may be hard to live with, but you can't squelch his personality without taking away that undefinable something that makes him unique. Now, I don't mean that you should let a kid run roughshod over you, wild all the time. No. But some kids from the time of their birth are just naturally more active than others, and a certain amount of this kind of "busyness" can be a good thing. This is the kind of child we call "upbeat." Naturally, when such a child gets out of hand, that over-aggressiveness has to be rechanneled into other directions. Some of that rambunctiousness has got to go, but only some of it. Give such a *child more to do*. Keep him occupied, don't hesitate to pile chores on him to absorb some of that excess energy. But don't try to melt all kids down to the same metal. A sensitive child is always going to remain sensitive, and there's nothing you can, or should, do to change that. The rambunctious child has a lot of hustle. Give him something to hustle about to pull down that rambunctiousness. Above all, try to cultivate whatever is unique in the child and to rechannel that superfluous energy. It's the reverse of trying to give the tractable child a little more get-up-and-go.

# IV
# Defecating and Other Natural Functions

As a child, I remember going to the movies and wondering how come none of the actors or actresses ever seemed to go to the bathroom. Not once did I see a toilet on the screen, only washbasins, bathtubs, and showers. I got the feeling that movie stars were very different from me and my family, or else that going to the bathroom was something dirty. I wouldn't be surprised if you had the same experience.

When I got older, I got smarter. I realized that everybody, even movie stars, had to go to the bathroom. Bowels must be moved and bladders emptied. These are natural functions for everybody. They aren't dirty, but they are very private activities, and they aren't esthetic in any way, shape, or form. Feces and urine are waste products that have to be eliminated, and so they tend to be seen as "dirty." In fact, there are lots of special "dirty" words to describe these processes and their products.

A child who has not yet learned to control these natural functions will soil and wet himself, and his parents have to pretend that they don't mind at all when actually they're mad as hell when they have to clean up the kid. Well, it *is* a messy job. Parents have to grin and bear it, but they'd have to be crazy to like mopping up their kid's mess. The point I'm trying to make is that these waste products *are* offensive (which is why the bathroom spray business is a multimillion dollar industry), but there is nothing offensive about a child's need to relieve himself.

Nevertheless, I think that most parents still feel a sense of shame about the natural functions. They do become embarrassed.

Maybe it's because they were conditioned by the movies, or because they have to contend with the child's messing and feel guilty about resenting the job. No matter. Parents have a right to these feelings.

Kids, however, get turned on by whatever is forbidden, private or "dirty." They get a big charge out of using words like "shit" and "piss," and get an even bigger charge from shocking their parents with their vocabulary. Well, so what if they do? Personally, I'd be more concerned about a kid who calls the product of elimination "feces" than I would about one who calls it "shit." Using the "dirty" term is part of growing up in a society that generally considers a reference to these natural functions impolite and improper.

Children do have to learn to control their natural functions and to recognize the unwritten rules of good social behavior. Some do go way overboard in rebelling against such proprieties. But parents must be more patient and less bashful about such behavior. Consider this chapter a brief survival manual for parents whose children do not share their sensitivity about the natural functions.

*What can you do with a child who refuses to do anything on the toilet, then soils his pants the minute he's taken off the seat?*

Stop putting the child on the toilet at scheduled times each day. This practice will only reinforce the child's habit of soiling *after* being removed. It is not encouraging him to move his bowels on the seat. Instead, leave him alone, let him soil his pants. Then, after he's soiled, pick him up or lead him to the toilet very casually and have him sit there a while. This will encourage him to *complete* the movement. Once he becomes accustomed to completing his bowel movements this way, he'll begin to feel more comfortable about sitting on the toilet. When he feels comfortable about sitting there and sees how pleased you are, then he's ready to be trained. That's the time to start getting him to the toilet before he soils. I've used this technique to train dozens of hard-to-handle kids, including many who were severely retarded or disturbed. It's a positive nonpunitive way to establish a reasonable association between being on the pot and eliminating.

*Shouldn't a second-grader know better than to let wind in company?*

He should. The next time he lets wind, say to him quietly, "Go to the bathroom when you have to do that." But be sure not to let others hear you. It's important that you don't embarrass the child even though he has embarrassed you. Just don't feel too embarrassed. The other guests have probably been through similar experiences with their children. When you find the right opportunity, take your child aside and explain to him that some things must be done privately. Tell him, "When your stomach makes a noise, you can't help it. But when your tooshy wants to make a noise, learn to hold it in just like you hold in making doody." Now, I've used euphemisms here because you may prefer to talk this way to your child. It might be better, though, to be more direct and use words like "fart" or "shit" if this is the language he understands best. Don't pussyfoot around. Talk his language if you want to get your message across. In these matters, a father is generally more effective with a son, and a mother with a daughter.

*What makes a five-year-old stick jelly beans and nuts up her anus and vagina?*

She is curious about those openings in her body, so she's doing some exploring. When I was a very small boy, I stuck a bean up my nose and neither my mama nor my daddy knew about it. A few months later I began to have trouble breathing. I was taken to a doctor who discovered that the bean had sprouted and was interfering with my breathing. He took out the sprout and I was fine again. Now, why did I shove the bean up my nose instead of up my backside? Because I was more curious about my nostrils, I guess. But many children, like this little girl, are more imaginative. They're more interested in exotic openings like their anus and vagina. Nothing will sprout in the anus because whatever is shoved up there will probably come out naturally. Poking objects up the vagina could be more dangerous. You have to teach this little girl not to do these things. How? By telling her what these openings are for. Instruct her that the vagina is for urinating and the anus for defecating, that the urine and feces come *out* of those openings. Explain that shoving things inside will prevent the urine and feces from coming out, and that she'll feel uncomfortable. You can say, "Jelly beans and nuts belong in your mouth, honey, where you can taste them and chew them and enjoy them more." Don't be ashamed to speak to her about such things, and don't be afraid to leave her alone on the toilet. She might want to do some exploring with her fingers. It won't do her any harm. It's just her way of testing what you've told her, and it'll help her become aware of how her body works.

*Is there anything amusing about a ten-year-old's enjoyment in writing notes to everyone—including his teacher—on toilet paper?*

Not to me, but the boy must find it amusing. This might be his way of telling his teacher and other people how little he thinks of them. Or maybe by signing his name on toilet paper he's indicating how little he thinks of himself. I mean, what properly belongs on toilet paper? Not your signature! I've known kids who thought it a great joke to wrap their feces up in toilet paper with a big blue ribbon and present it to someone as a "gift." That's a child's idea of a dirty joke. Where adults verbalize their dirty jokes, kids sometimes like to act them out. All such jokes represent aggressive feelings that are expressed by having a laugh at somebody else's expense. Sometimes, though, preoccupation with things associated with defecation suggests deeper, more personal feelings. There was a boy I knew who used to wait in the road for a farmer's truckload of fertilizer to come by. Then he'd jump into the mess, smear himself with it, and yell, "See, I'm shit! I'm shit!" He wasn't trying to be funny. He was trying to tell the world what he thought of himself. So when a boy writes notes on toilet paper, it could clue you in to how he feels about himself and other people. You know your son. Does he lack self-esteem? Does he dislike authority figures such as his teacher, or is he fearful of them? While you ponder these questions, pay a little more notice to him and buy him a box of stationery with his name printed on it.

*Would you call a boy who urinates all over his brother's possessions sick?*

I'd certainly guess that he has a real hate on for his brother. Can you think of some reason why? Is his brother the favorite son? Does he do better in school? There might be a subtle kind of discrimination in the home of which you're unaware. But this boy might be very sensitive and feel he's being cheated out of something: affection, intelligence, almost anything. Why would he pee on his brother's possessions? To show his contempt for his brother, to humiliate him. Also, to infuriate his parents so that he can be punished for doing such mean things and having such mean feelings. You might call him "sick." But if this is the only symptom of his sickness, I'd just say he's extra sensitive and is pleading for help. Punishment isn't going to help. He should be told firmly, "Don't do that again!" The dirtied things should be picked up and washed, and the victimized brother should be mollified and told to ignore the matter. If the incident is repeated, handle it the same way. Keep your cool. When the boy ceases to get a rise out of the family, he will be likely to stop acting up this way. Give him more of your time and attention even though you think he's getting his rightful share. Bring your other son into your confidence and explain the technique you're using. You have to make him feel important enough not to resent the extra time and attention being given his brother, whom he sees as the "bad boy." He can be of great help in making him a "good boy" if he is involved actively in the family's handling of the situation. But if he's too young to welcome the responsibility, don't involve him. His resentments will subside as his brother's attitude grows more respectful.

*Is the child who makes in his pants, then hides the turds in a desk drawer or wastebasket, psychotic?*

Possibly, if it happens often and if the child is in the upper grades of elementary school. I'd come to grips with this pretty quickly if I were the parent and just say, "Hey, take this shit and throw it down the toilet, just like everybody else does." By using a coarse word, I'm taking some of the edge off the child's embarrassment. By telling him casually what to do, I'm letting him know that a lot of other people mess their pants. You see, the way a child handles defecation generally serves as a bellwether of his overall emotional well-being. I've seen mixed-up fourteen-year-olds flush their dirty pants down the toilet and hide their turds under beds, pillows, even in the refrigerator. This kind of furtive behavior is a red light to serious maladjustment. So I say, play down the problem. Kids shouldn't be so embarrassed about defecation—even accidents that cause them to mess their pants—to the point where they find it necessary to hide their leavings. For purely physical reasons, digestive systems can go wrong and cause a loss of self-control. It happens to everybody at some time, to mama and daddy, to the teacher, even to judges and movie stars. A parent shouldn't react by saying, "Oh, that's all right, there's nothing wrong," but he shouldn't go to extremes either. Look upon it as no different than your daughter coming home from school menstruating, and she's a mess. You would tell her, "Go take a bath, honey, and clean up." You don't make the child smell it, eat it, or sleep with it. Check around to see if there isn't too much concern at home about the private functions. I've known parents who ran the water in the basin to conceal their urinating. This is too much.

*Should a parent be concerned about a child who loves to take enemas?*

I think so. I know I would be. Sometimes, parents become too occupied with their children's bowel movements. They keep asking: "Did you move your bowels today? Did you make a lot this morning? Was it hard to make tonight?" Now, not everybody has to go to the bathroom every day. This is a myth. The system has to be kept clear but this doesn't necessarily involve a daily bowel movement. A lot of kids find it normal to go every other day. Unfortunately, some mamas get worried when their kids miss a movement one day and rush to give them enemas. It's not wise. There's something else, too. A lot of concerned mamas never stop wiping their kids' behinds. These kids become stimulated by the wiping and get to like it. They often try pushing harder to "make more" for mama. I'd guess that a child who loves to take enemas would be one who's taken so many enemas, or who's had so much anal stimulation, that he's become dependent on the enema to have a bowel movement—and feels pressed to have that movement. I'd say to the parents of such kids: "Relax. Kids don't need enemas so frequently and in fact shouldn't get them very often. If they're constipated, let them be constipated for a few days. Then try a laxative. If they must have an enema, teach them how to handle it themselves." It boils down to the fact that some parents simply worry too much —some about their kids being too fat, some about their kids not being fat enough, and others about their kids not being "regular" in their bowel habits. My advice is to throw the enema away. The child will survive better, and so will you.

*Why in the world would a child enjoy sniffing her dog's behind? It's nauseating!*

Sure it is, but not to her. She's probably playing a role,

identifying with the dog for one reason or another. I once treated a little girl who really thought she was a dog. She walked, ate, barked, just like a dog. She wanted to be a dog, in fact, because she had lost her faith in human beings. And she sniffed her dog's behind because that's what she saw other dogs do. Well, I had to reestablish her faith in people again to make her give up playing the role of a dog. It took many months and a great deal of patient understanding. Now, I don't think your daughter is anywhere near this stage. Still, what she is doing is a "no-no." When she sniffs her dog's behind, she is hiding from the world, demeaning herself. She is probably a very sensitive child. You are going to need lots of patience and understanding to break her of this habit. But you begin by putting your foot down. You tell her, "No, you don't do that. You want to sniff something? All right, sniff at these flowers, this cake I just made, your daddy's pipe tobacco." I'd even consider it progress if she sniffed her armpits. It's better than sniffing a dog's backside. This is bizarre behavior and you have to say no to it. After the "No" comes love and understanding. Remember that both love and understanding are communicated by saying "No" as well as "Yes." It's part of discipline, and every child requires it. It might be necessary for you to take the dog away. Don't become overconcerned about it if you do. Your child will get over it. If you don't put your foot down, she may even go so far as to try to have sex with the dog. Say "No." You must get her back to relating to people.

*How do you discourage a nine-year-old from washing her hands in the toilet—in other people's urine, even feces—and who relishes the smell of a toilet, rushing in after others have relieved themselves?*

Well, you can tell her it's unsanitary behavior, but it won't work. You have to do the unexpected, something far-out. Make her the queen of the toilet if she likes the bathroom that much. Have her show party guests to the bathroom. Put her in charge of seeing to it that there's enough soap and towels and toilet paper there. Take away the need for her to be devious. Unkindle the fire by making the bathroom a natural part of the home environment. Put her in charge of the room. After a while, this role will become a chore, unpleasant. And that's what you have to do, make the bathroom a perfectly normal place to visit but not the most pleasant room in the house. I'd go a little bit further and let the girl share the bathroom with you, her mama. When she's on the toilet, you knock on the door and go in to comb your hair or brush your teeth. This helps to take away the fascination the bathroom seems to have for her and serves to make it commonplace instead of a special attraction full of mystery. This is her hang-up, you see; the bathroom has taken on a kind of mystique for her. Maybe there's too much privacy in your home, and the bathroom has attained a kind of sacred quality. Well, there's a limit to privacy in a family. A bathroom is not an altar. I think it's healthy for a girl of nine to pop into the bathroom when her mama's in the tub, or even on the pot. Why not? If you take her to the bathroom in a department store, you're going to share the bathroom with her. Do the same at home. She'll feel that going to the bathroom is a natural thing to do and she'll lose the urge to make explorations there.

*There's something strange about a boy who likes to fart into a bottle, give it to others, then giggle when they open it and smell the contents. Should such a boy be punished?*

I wouldn't punish him. I wouldn't try to look into this too deeply either. Nor would I shove the bottle in his face and say, "Here, you smell it." This boy knows it smells to high heaven, that's why he's done what he's done. I'd simply treat this youngster as being very bratty because he knows what he's doing. He reminds me of the kid who puts a tack on teacher's chair. Even adults do similarly foolish things. I just read about a man who thought it fun to sprinkle LSD all over the food and in the drinks of the guests attending a big party. This youngster is something of a practical jokester and he has to be put down. I'd take him aside when I discovered his "trick" and tell him bluntly, "This is a lousy trick to play on people. Don't ever do it again!" There's no need for you to be embarrassed by this kind of behavior. It's within the boy's ability to control such behavior. Here's a case where you, the parent, wonder if there aren't deeper reasons for the child's behavior. There may very well be such reasons. But I don't think you have to be concerned with such possibilities. I look upon this, plain and simple, as brattiness. Your only job here is to make the youngster know that you won't countenance such behavior. You don't have to tell him why, he knows why. And because he knows, you are in the enviable position of being able to simply say, "I want no more of this. Behave yourself." Disregard his mumbling and grumbling. He'll never tell you so, but I think he'll secretly be pleased that you were so decisive, and he'll be much the stronger for it.

# V
# Physical Hangups

Some kids have less going for them physically than others. They might have bad eyesight or be totally blind, be hard of hearing or totally deaf, be sickly or suffer a gross deformity, or they might simply be "ugly ducklings." Such youngsters are often hard to love and almost always hard to raise, but few parents will admit it. Many blame themselves for their child's defects, regarding such imperfections as reflections of their own inadequacies. I've known mothers and fathers so sensitive about their kids' handicaps that I could see a grimace of pain cross their faces every time they looked at their son or daughter. Theirs is a sadness that never leaves.

I've also known mothers and fathers who couldn't bear to look at their severely handicapped children because the sight was too upsetting. Now, if we are going to make sense together, let us face up to the fact that a physically defective child is likely to make a parent feel guilty, perhaps ashamed, and even disgusted.

So what of it?

Have you ever seen photographs of those pitifully crippled thalidomide babies with missing limbs and twisted little bodies? Were they pleasant to look at? Didn't you feel sick looking at those pictures? The reaction is only natural. But these weren't your babies, so you didn't feel guilty. And you didn't feel ashamed. You could turn your back on them and go back to your business, feeling grateful that your kids were all in one piece.

The mother who loves her defective child is hardest on herself. She won't permit herself the luxury of resenting the pain that the child's disability has caused her to suffer. But it is her love for the child that is tying her up into knots emotionally by denying her the privilege of letting such resentment, anger, and disappointment surface. She can look at the thalidomide baby without being bothered by such feelings because that baby is not hers, makes no demands upon her, and there is no interchange of love.

Children suffer more from a parent's reluctance to own up to negative feelings, a reluctance that prevents such feelings from being discharged in healthy ways. Instead, parents sometimes *pretend* to love the child at times when they don't truly feel like loving him at all. They might overpamper the youngster, often at the expense of the well children in the family ("You should know better than to pick on your poor crippled sister, there isn't anything wrong with *you!*"). Such an attitude is sure to turn the siblings—and often the other parent—against the handicapped child. When this occurs, the youngster is likely to become emotionally damaged, and, eventually, the whole family will be victimized.

It is better for parents to be honest with themselves, as I hope this chapter makes plain. They will then be able to deal honest feelings to their child and give only the best of themselves as parents.

*Can a physically deformed child be raised as a normal child?*

Sure, but a parent has to work hard to remove the stigma of being different. My first student was a nine-year-old girl, nearly blind with cataracts, almost totally deaf, and suffering from a cardiac condition. She was a mess, ugly to look at and terribly disturbed as a result of her physical disabilities. She wept, she shrieked, she hit. Well, I began to have that little girl treated by medical specialists to remove her most obvious physical deficiencies. An ear specialist brought up her hearing by more than fifty percent; an ophthalmologist removed the cataracts; and a cardiologist performed open-heart surgery. After she recovered from these procedures, I had her hair cut, dressed her up prettily, and did everything I could to make her stop feeling different from other kids. I knew—and she knew—that she would never win first prize in a beauty contest, but how many girls can? What we did know was that she could make a decent life for herself once she started feeling like a human being instead of a freak of nature. I had to spend a lot of time with her, show interest in her, and help her along to make the most of her capabilities. And you know something? She stopped feeling like an ugly misfit with nothing to live for and began to behave like a normal, healthy, and attractive child. When she learned to like herself more, she became more likeable. Any child with a physical deformity needs the same kind of care and attention to head off emotional problems and lead a normal life, at least within the limits of the child's disability.

*How do you make a preteenager understand that the pimples on her face are nothing and should be ignored?*

The pimples aren't "nothing" and she knows it. You might be able to convince her that a pimple on her backside is nothing because nobody can see it there. But you can't hide a pimply face. It's a good idea to make little of such blemishes but it's unreasonable to expect a child to ignore their existence. Girls—and boys, too—place high value on their appearance when they enter their teens. This is the time when they begin to show interest in attracting the opposite sex. A bad case of adolescent acne can make them feel very self-conscious. Of course, their sense of shame is generally all out of proportion to the situation. So what can a girl's mother do? Well, without denying the problem, she can reassure the youngster that pimples aren't permanent and will disappear soon after adolescence. This isn't going to make the child feel any happier about her appearance, but it might make her feel less concerned so that she'll learn to live with the situation. See that she keeps her face clean and doesn't pick at the pimples. Don't, however, keep harping on her about these things because this could aggravate her emotional conflict. See that she dresses nicely, wears her hair in style, and when she's invited to parties, make sure she goes. If, despite all your logic and persuasion, she remains unconvinced that her pimples will ever clear up, have your doctor speak to her. He might be able to show her before-and-after photographs of kids like herself whose pimples did clear up with time as you assured her they would.

*Should a sickly eight-year-old who suffers from allergies, earaches, and constant discomfort be punished for teasing his playmates unmercifully?*

You don't have to punish him, but you should certainly correct him. If you don't, he'll never learn how to discipline himself. A sickly child will quickly take advantage of his special situation once he realizes that mama will defend him no matter what he does. Mama may understandably be fed up and want to slam the child across the room. She certainly wouldn't be justified in acting on that impulse, but she's entitled to feel like doing so. In fact, if she didn't, I'd think there was something wrong with her. The point is, she can feel mean without acting mean. But what happens is that mama feels ashamed for having such an impulse. She thinks a mother has no business even *feeling* mean. So she goes in the opposite direction, becoming more tolerant, more forgiving, and more of a pushover for the child. In trying to do the right thing, she does the wrong thing. This doesn't do the child any good. He must learn that his sickness doesn't give him special privileges as a human being. If he continues to tease his playmates, he'll be disliked. He won't be able to make friends and then he'll really feel like a misfit. And you know something else? He'll blame his mother for it. A sickly child, especially one who's prone to allergies, will do much better if he's disciplined kindly but firmly, when it's necessary. This proper discipline will teach him to master his instincts. In time this will make him feel superior to his sickliness and will elevate his self-image.

*When your little boy cries to you that his friends joke about his looking like he comes from outer space (because of a harelip and a funny way of talking), what do you do?*

You give the child a big kiss smack on the harelip, and tell him he came from right inside your body because his mama and daddy wanted a little boy exactly like him! And tell him that if he hears such foolishness again to laugh at their silly joke even if it isn't funny just to make them feel good. This approach will help counter some of the damage to the child's self-esteem. Don't indicate that you feel sorry for the youngster, even though his tears are breaking your heart, because that will only teach him to feel sorry for himself. Treat the matter as unemotionally as possible. You can be sure that any kid who talks this way to your child is no friend. But it's healthier for your boy to learn to shake off such comments rather than to shun the kids who make them. I know that mothers are very sensitive to criticism about a child with a disfigurement. All right, but if I were that mother, I'd say to myself: What do I care what some ignorant kid or person says! I'll bet these kids are far from perfect. If they don't have physical hang-ups, I'm damned sure they've got emotional hang-ups that make a harelip seem like a blessing in comparison! I'd remember, too, that one out of fifteen children are born with harelips, cleft palates, missing fingers, or other birth defects. But I would hock everything I owned, if necessary, to pay a plastic surgeon to correct the disfigurement. This should be the family's number-one priority, not just for the child's well-being, but for the suffering parents as well.

*How do you prevent an epileptic child's convulsive seizures from contaminating his brother and sister?*

Convulsive seizures aren't infectious. You don't "catch" epilepsy from an epileptic. Brother and sister won't be con taminated by the convulsions, but they could be affected emotionally if the epileptic child is treated like an outcast because of his handicap. The way to keep everyone healthy is for the whole family to recognize that one of their members suffers from an illness that sometimes manifests itself in very dramatic and frightening episodes. Everyone should be instructed by his physician on how to keep the epileptic child from hurting himself during a seizure. This will take the mystery and fear out of such episodes so that they won't seem any more formidable than, say, a bellyache. You have to handle a situation like this in a matter-of-fact, straightforward way to avoid the possibility of panic and anxiety. The family attitude should be one of goodwill, with the parents setting the example for the other kids. The same approach holds true for the family with a youngster who's a diabetic, a cardiac, or whatever. Such a child should not inspire fear or be made an object of pity. It should be explained that he's different only because he has a medical problem, and that everybody should pitch in to give him his medicine when he needs it. Simple as that.

*If your mongoloid child increasingly gets on your nerves, how can you show love for the child?*

Sometimes you can't. I think you may have reached the point where home may not be the best place for your child. I'd say that until about eight years old, mongoloid children should stay at home. They're very lovable until about that time when they begin to be different from other children. These are still nice, wonderful kids but their appearance becomes grotesque. Certain physical characteristics begin to predominate. When that happens, it is usually best for the child—and for the parents—for the youngster to be placed with his peers, kids like himself, in a residential center if you can afford it, or in a state institution if you can't. Although such facilities, especially those run by the state, may be less than ideal, they have improved greatly in their ability to care for such kids. Now, this may seem a cruel thing to do, and it isn't customary for me to suggest taking a child out of his home; but in the case of the mongoloid child it may be the most thoughtful thing to do. You confess that the child gets on your nerves a lot of times. Well, in view of your feelings, can you continue to cope? Do you have the necessary devotion to do right by your child? Is this youngster getting on the nerves of his brothers and sisters as well? I know that many parents consider it selfish to take their child out of their home, but keeping this child home isn't fair to the child. Although he is part of the day-to-day life of his normal family, he is unable to participate equally in their activities. He becomes an outsider, like a fifth wheel. Is this fair to him? I don't think so.

*Is it healthy for a normal child to play with kids who are deaf, dumb, blind, crippled, or otherwise handicapped?*

It can be very healthy if the youngster spends a portion of his time with kids less fortunate than himself, or different from himself. This applies whether they're handicapped, represent different races or religions, or come from the other side of the tracks. One learns something from the other, the same way the city boy learns from the country boy and vice versa. The experience could serve to make the child more tolerant and understanding. However, if he spends all of his time in the exclusive company of children who cannot meet him on his level, it is unhealthy. I would suspect that the child finds difficulty relating to his peers and finds gratification only in being with kids less capable than himself. Now, there are some children who need this kind of gratification in order to survive emotionally. They build up their own self-esteem by helping those less fortunate, and some choose careers that permit them to receive such gratification throughout their adult life. Fine. People like that are irreplaceable and enrich our society. But similar good works are done by people who can also relate comfortably to their equals—and their superiors. This is healthier and even more satisfying. If this were my child, I'd show pleasure and approval about his interest in playing with handicapped kids, but I'd encourage him to give more of his time to playing with kids like himself. I'd do the same if he spent all his time with just one friend; I'd encourage him to spend time in other kids' company as well. By restricting himself to one kind of companion, he misses out on social learning opportunities. That kind of education is just as necessary as schooling.

*How in God's name do you explain to a child who's hunchbacked and a dwarf that he's different and will always be?*

You don't have to explain this. He knows he's different; he lives it. Going into lengthy explanations will emphasize that difference. You have to be careful not to get into long involved explanations that could reach the stage of "protesting too much," because at that point you'll begin to project feelings of shame. As for the future, the youngster will recognize for himself that he is always going to be different. You needn't and shouldn't volunteer such information. But if he asks you point-blank, "Mama, will I always be like this?" then you must tell him, "Yes, son, that's a burden you're going to have to bear. But you're going to have a good life despite it. I'm going to help you, daddy's going to help you, and you're going to help yourself." This isn't easy for a parent to do. Often, there's a tendency to hope that some miracle will make the hump on the child's back disappear and that one day he'll wake up tall and straight. There's an emotional urge to tell the child, "Of course you're just like everybody else." But when you give in to that urge, you only fool yourself, never the child. He'll think to himself, "Don't give me that crap, mama. I'm ugly and you know it!" It's almost better to say, "Yes, you are ugly but only physically, and that doesn't stop us from loving you. You're beautiful in lots of other ways. We already know this, and you have to give others a chance to find out for themselves." There are many parents in the same boat, and it's good for them as well as for their kids to find each other and get together now and then. Your doctor should be able to arrange such acquaintances.

*Is there some way to change the attitude of grandparents— whose distaste for their handicapped granddaughter is obvious —without hurting their feelings?*

Their feelings come second to those of the child. If you, the parent, begin worrying too much about hurting them, you'll find yourself in such an emotional bind that you'll become desperate to find an outlet for your frustrations. The most likely one to suffer will be your little girl because she's more defenseless and less threatening than her grandparents. This is why you *must* give priority to the child's feelings. If it's your parents who find the child's handicap not to their taste, you should speak to them; if they are your in-laws, your spouse should speak to them. Just say, "This is my child and I love her. I wish you did, too, but you don't have to. Please try, though, not to criticize her or turn her away. It will be better for you not to bother with her at all if she upsets you." It isn't just the handicapped child, but any child, who has to be protected in this way. Grandparents can dislike a child for reasons other than a handicap. There may be emotional conflict between you (or your spouse) and the grandparents. They raised their child their way; you're raising yours your way. Sometimes this results in a personality clash with the child the scapegoat. Whatever the reason, you might succeed in changing the grandparents' *attitude* to the little girl, or boy—simply by appealing to their better instincts—but this won't change their *feelings*. This can be accomplished only if the child herself manages to win them over. This is unlikely because the grandparents feel uncomfortable about her handicap, and so don't find her lovable. You're best off keeping them apart in consideration of the child's feelings.

*How do you keep a delicate child who's a hemophiliac from playing "dangerous" games that might hurt him?*

You don't keep him from them. You train him to protect himself. You tell him his problem the same as you would tell any child, "If you cross the street without looking both ways, you might be hit by a car." In this child's case, you say, "If you aren't careful with that knife, you might cut yourself," or "If you want to play roughhouse, protect yourself against getting bruised." You must make it clear to him—but without arousing undue alarm—that he has to guard against cuts or bruises that will make him bleed. Unless he is made aware that he has a very special kind of handicap, he'll fail to take precautions. It's not the sort of handicap that can be brushed aside or otherwise made insignificant. On the other hand, it could be very damaging emotionally to overstate the case. This is why I believe in letting such kids play, but in making them understand that they must learn to take care of themselves. The child, no matter how young, must be made a party to his disability. This is a role your doctor should play. It helps when the doctor takes the child into his confidence and explains the problem scientifically to the extent of the child's ability to understand. This tends to give the child confidence in his ability to cope with his problem. It's the parents' job to smooth the emotional edges of the child's concern. It's a tough job because the parents have to take the day-to-day anxiety onto their own shoulders. Hemophilia can't be taken lightly. The prevention of physical injury must take precedence over anything else. But emotional concern can be minimized by allowing the child normal play activities if he is willing and able to take care of himself.

# VI
# Lying, Cheating, and Stealing

By the time a child has learned to walk and talk and understand what is said to him, parents generally feel he's passed the age of innocence. Those stories he tells about strangers coming into his room at night and tearing up the curtains (that mama knows he himself tore) are interpreted as falsehoods. If he tells such tall tales to strangers, they are apt to regard him as a little liar, a child of poor moral character.

But there is nothing morally deceitful in these stories. They are part of the child's fantasy life, part of growing up, one of the methods by which the child learns to master his environment. He finds the real world threatening and so he conjures up his own make-believe world protection, then little by little he gains confidence enough to leave his fantasies behind him and take on the real world. All the while, he knows his stories are make-believe and expects grown-ups to understand and trust him. It is not a time for parents to try to wring the "truth" out of him, or to spank him, or to issue a lecture on the difference between "right" and "wrong."

Even in later years, parents must be careful how they handle suspected lies. If a child is misjudged or shamed into a confession about an inconsequential lie, the only thing he'll learn will be to lie more convincingly in the future. He will also commence to lose trust in his parents. This means that if he should ever again lie, cheat, or steal—and regret the deception—he will be reluctant to turn to his parents for help. That is when parents lose control of their child.

I don't want to be misunderstood. Some kids are liars, cheats, and thieves when they are old enough to know better. At what age does this happen? That depends on the child. For some, it could be twelve; for others, it could be as young as eight. Delinquency begins when incidents of lying, cheating, and stealing are repeated until they become an integral part of the child's general behavior.

Parents have to use all the resources at their command to intervene early enough in the child's development to rechannel these unhealthy interests and impulses to healthier outlets. It is a demanding job, but I think parents can do it better than anybody else—if they know what they're doing. I hope you'll find some ideas in this chapter on how to accomplish these things.

*Is it really stealing when a child takes pennies and chewing gum from his mother's purse?*

I'm sure you know it is but just don't like to admit it. However, it is a very special kind of stealing. He is taking things that belong exclusively to his mother, some part of her in a way. Maybe he is simply taking love where he can find it: in his mama's purse. If you think this might be the case, that the child is seeking more of your attention and affection, then don't bawl him out or turn him over to his daddy for punishment. Just let him know that you're on to him. Say to him, "I didn't know you wanted chewing gum but I see you went to my bag for some. Shall I buy you a pack of your own so you won't have to take mine?" Assure the child that all he has to do is ask for things, gum, pennies, or whatever, and if you're *able* to, you'll give them to him. When you do give him things, put them into his hand; don't simply put them on his desk or bureau. Let him feel your touch as part of the giving. If this child *feels* deprived, even though you don't think he is, don't force him to give back the pennies stolen from your bag. You can't take something away from a child who already feels deprived. Sometimes, without the parents realizing it, there is a lot of talk at home about not having enough money. A mother might say to a child, "Here's a dime I kept out of our food money so you can have an ice cream cone." She means well, but the child begins to feel the pinch, and this could motivate him to steal. In any case, the purse should not be hidden from the child. It should be left in the open as always, not as temptation, but as an indication of trust.

*How do you stop a first-grader from continually lying, always telling you "I can do this, I can do that," when he really can't do these things at all?*

What he's trying to tell you is that he'd like to try. He wants to earn your approval by showing you how capable he is and keeps overestimating his ability. Well, is he lying? Yes, but more to himself than to you, and all in good faith. Many kids do this: the little boy who watches his daddy hammer a nail and says, "I can do that as good as you," or the little girl who watches her mama knitting and says, "Oh, that's easy, I can do it even faster." You give such a child the chance to try. The boy might bang his finger; the girl might stick herself with the needle. Then you comfort them and encourage them to try again. You don't cluck over their failures and mistakes with an I-told-you-so like "See, you were bragging again, you were lying, you don't know how after all." Such kids like to bite off more than they can chew, and you have to help them to be successful. Many such children behave like this in the classroom, raising their hands just to look smart and then not knowing the answers. If this happens, their teachers might lose faith in them, and this would be bad for the kids. They have to learn at home to think before they act. If they're allowed to try, and fail, then try again and again until they succeed, they'll learn their lesson and will stop overrating their abilities by "lying." Until that happens, be glad that they are motivated to be winners and nurture that motivation with care.

*Why would an honor student humiliate her parents by cheating on a test? Even her teacher was shocked!*

It may surprise you to know that most cheating in school is done by honor students. It's done because the competition among these students is very keen. They aren't worried about failure; they're concerned about coming out on top. To do anything less is tantamount to being disgraced. It's all part of the academic rat race to get high grades, make the best colleges, and be a "somebody." Average students don't have this incentive so they don't cheat as much. They might cheat in matters that interest them—a ballgame, getting the best of someone in a swap, a bake-a-cake contest—but they aren't hungry enough to cheat for higher grades. You may discover that this isn't the first time this youngster has cheated, only the first time she's been caught. And you know something else? There are many teachers who pretend not to notice such cheating because they're equally anxious for their honor students to do well. The best way to find out why your daughter cheated is just to ask her. Don't scold her for embarrassing you. She's embarrassed, too. Instead, use this opportunity to become more familiar with her goals, and with yours. Perhaps she's demanding too much of herself because she wants to make her parents proud of her, and thinks she can accomplish this only by excelling. Now's your chance to tell her that you're proud of her just for working to the full extent of her ability, and that she doesn't have to top everybody else in class to prove herself. Treat the cheating as an isolated incident even if you suspect it's happened before. By clearing the air in this way, I think you'll be spared future embarrassment.

*Should your six-year-old be allowed to say what she thinks even though her bad manners hurt people's feelings?*

I get the impression that this little girl is less fresh than she is ingenuous, thoroughly honest. She hasn't yet learned the social grace called tact. In other words, she doesn't know how to tell polite lies out of consideration for other people's feelings. She's probably outspoken enough to say quite innocently to relatives and adult friends: "You have big ears," "You're awful old," "Your breath smells phooey," things like that. Well, this could very well embarrass a parent, but the tactless child just isn't ready to assume a "civilized" role by either keeping her mouth shut, or lying, in order to avoid making social blunders. You shouldn't punish her for this "oversight." You shouldn't apologize for her remarks, either. Just shrug them off with a smile, suggesting in effect that kids will be kids. However, since it is necessary for her to learn to be responsive to our social codes, begin teaching her consideration for other people's feelings. I say this with a certain reluctance because it hurts me to see kids give up their wonderful innocence. On the other hand, the child is going to be hurt if she doesn't behave in a socially acceptable way. Explain to the child that she can think however she likes, and can express her feelings to you without concealing them in any way, but that because most people are offended easily, she can't always tell them how she feels about the way they look or act. Say to her, "Look, honey, you'd feel bad if somebody told you that you had big ears. Other people feel bad too. You can think it all you want, but don't say it because you'll hurt their feelings." She'll catch on. All kids do. But please don't teach her to tell her homely aunt, "You're beautiful." That would be phony. Just teach her to say nothing. That would be considerate.

*When you catch your young son forging his father's name to a check, what do you do?*

Anything you do is better than nothing. If you do nothing, that's equivalent to condoning the forgery; ultimately, society will handle the problem for you. That could be very unpleasant for the boy and for the whole family because society holds that writing a forged check for ten dollars is worse than stealing ten dollars. In the eyes of the law, this is a worse crime. As soon as you discover the forgery, you permit the check to clear to protect the boy from possible prosecution, but you take the matter up with him at once. Tell him: "This is something you must never, never do," and demand your money back from him. Now, I'm wondering why this young man forged his father's name to a check. Most of the time, such kids have expensive tastes and either don't want to work or just won't wait until they can save enough money to buy whatever it is they want. Up to the time that a boy hasn't yet reached his teens, this might be called a prank. By the time of the teens, sometimes sooner, though, it is generally a sign of a character disorder. I have a feeling that certain behavioral lapses were overlooked by the parents of such youngsters, perhaps written off as "harmless." Generally, these kids feel they've been deprived. This can sometimes be translated as meaning that they haven't been given as much as they wanted. Usually, what they lacked wasn't money, but attention, affection, or approval. This may have occurred because they weren't easy to get along with and, to make them easier to live with, the parents allowed themselves to be manipulated by them. I think that now you have to speak out your true feelings and give the boy a chance to open up.

*How do you handle a rebellious child who says the older generation lies and cheats, so why should he be different?*

Well, if this isn't true of you—or if you can convince him that it isn't, even though it is—then you say, "Some do, not me." Just be sure he believes you. Otherwise, you put yourself in the position of saying, "Look, I drink and I get drunk, but I don't want you to behave that way," or "Okay, I'm coughing because I smoke too much, so let that be a lesson to you not to smoke." You have to set an example, you see. If you brag about how you fudge on your taxes, or rationalize your decision to pocket the extra change the supermarket gave you by mistake, you make yourself vulnerable to this kind of rebellion. However, even the most upright parents sometimes find, to their great surprise, that their child becomes rebellious to the point of declaring, "What's the good of being honest? Honesty doesn't get you anywhere!" In some cases, this is the rub-off of what's happening in society, not at home. It's a cry of despair from the child reflecting awful disappointment in the kind of morality he'd been led to believe was respected and rewarded. But the newspapers and television tell him a much different story. Look upon such a child's attitude not as rebellion but as despair. Don't lecture him, don't deny the headlines. Allow the youngster to let off steam. Tell him, "Sure, there are lots of crooks around and some of them do get away with murder, but most of them go to jail. When you get older, you'll discover that their lives are all messed up no matter how much they make, how much they get away with. And if you don't want to grow up in a dishonest world, you have to be honest yourself." But don't press the point. There's a fine line between "good business practice" and dishonesty, and in time your youngster will learn to tread this line by himself.

*It's pretty embarrassing to have other parents whisper that your child is a tattletale. How do you deal with a little tattletale?*

The first thing you have to be sure of is that this child is really tattling. If it happens in school, there might be an honor system that demands that students report anybody who is cheating. You can't call a kid a tattletale if he abides by the rules of an honor system. Then, too, you have to consider the possibility that the child has taken a test that means a lot to him and is highly competitive. Well, the system is such that he'll suffer if other kids cheated and so did better. That hurts him. So why should he keep quiet? Don't misunderstand me, I don't approve of tattling, but I think I should point out that there could be times when tattling is nothing more than playing according to the rules, or is a means of protecting one's own interests in a social setting that makes the stakes so very important. There's another kind of tattling that's akin to gossip. It takes on the aspect of a game played in secrecy. Your child comes home and says, "Hey, mom, wait'll you hear what happened!" Then he proceeds to give you some scuttlebutt about his friends or your friends. Well, the way to make him lose interest in such gossiping is to beat him to the punch. If you've a nose for gossip, do some tattling yourself before your child can do so. If you can't, then just listen and shrug off the information with a "Oh, I already knew that." This discourages further tattling. Generally, any child who runs to mama or anybody else to spill the beans on somebody is in search of approval from his listeners. Discourage this need by playing down such gossip when he brings it home and ask about his other activities.

*If a youngster cheats in games with a parent, or a brother or sister, should you let it pass?*

No. This child is too afraid of losing. There are times when it makes sense to let a youngster win to build his self-esteem, but this would be your doing. Here, however, the child is calling the shots, cheating for victory, and that isn't healthy. I always say, look for something to be thankful for, and you have that—you've caught the child cheating, you haven't been hoodwinked. That is something to be thankful for. If he was really slick, you would have no idea of what was going on. Because he's a bumbler, you're one up on him and can do something about the matter. What do you do? You say to him, "Son, if you want to play with me, play by the rules, win or lose. Remember, it's only a game. I'm playing my best and you should play your best. But let's not have anybody kid anybody in this game!" Lay it out as simply as that. Don't punish him, don't bawl him out, don't stop playing with him. Just let him know you're on to him. If you win, act pleased, but don't rub it in. If he wins, make a big thing of it, but not too big. Over a period of time, several games, try to arrive at a happy medium where neither victory nor defeat will be greeted with undue enthusiasm or scorn. Don't play games that are beyond the child's ability. Give him every chance to win fair and square, and congratulate him when he does. Be an interested bystander when he plays games with his friends. Notice if he cheats or gets into frequent arguments with his rival. When the game is over, talk to him. Show pleasure in his having played a good game, win or lose. If he was argumentative, tell him bluntly to cut it out, that other kids will resent it. Don't belabor it. He'll understand. After a while he'll stop cheating, no matter whom he plays with.

*How do you discipline a child who's a petty shoplifter?*

This is the hardest thing in the world to do. I've known parents who became so frustrated that they threatened to put their kids' hands in plaster casts. Some kids steal because they don't have very much. They want more and they don't care how they get things. Still, I know cases where parents gave such children more money and the kids continued to steal. Compulsive gamblers and kleptomaniacs share in common their need to get away with something. All right, then, I think you have to consider first what it is that the child steals, and then what he does with his loot. His stealing is petty, but are these things he needs or wants? Does he give them away like Robin Hood? Does he grab what's easy to grab or does he take risks, enjoying the thrill of getting away with something that isn't easy to get away with? All these questions bear on the kind of shoplifter he is. There's something else, too. I've known youngsters who stole, not for the sake of stealing, but for something they wanted, and in the hope that they would be caught and helped. I knew a young girl, for example, who shoplifted a bottle of aspirins in a supermarket and gulped them all down at once. She chose the time and place to steal and to attempt suicide so that she could be caught and given attention that she wasn't getting at home. Regardless of the reason behind the shoplifting, you must put a stop to that before doing anything else. Use all the rational arguments you can think of. Without being angry or punitive, go back to the store with the child and make him return what he's stolen, or have him pay for it, or work to pay it off. But stand by him. If he's arrested, stand by him and bail him out. The attention you give him, even by this devious route, may be enough to make him stop stealing.

*If you catch your child in lies—about his homework, his test grades, his personal habits like smoking pot—what can you do about such sneaky behavior?*

This is a child who is terribly fearful of punishment. That's why he keeps doing things behind your back. This sneakiness has probably been going on longer than you think. Don't heap a lot of blame upon yourself, because the reason for this youngster's sneakiness may lie with his extreme sensitivity and not really with the way you've raised him. Give him the benefit of every doubt. Consider the possibility that he may be expecting too much of himself, in which case he *would* lie about his grades. Say to him, "Just do your best, that's good enough for me, and it should be good enough for you, too." Reassurance is the best antidote for this kind of deception. In effect, you tell him that you accept him as he is, that's good enough for you. It means a lot to a troubled child. Now, about the pot. If he has told you that he smokes, you are already winning. That shows that he does trust you to understand. It doesn't mean he wants your approval to continue smoking pot, only that he wants your understanding. So don't beat him down if he tells you. But if he doesn't tell you, then confront him, tell him you suspect that he is smoking, and ask if he would tell you why. Let him talk out his feelings. Don't argue with him, just listen. Say to him, "Okay, so you're smoking. I wish you wouldn't continue because you can wind up in a helluva lot of trouble if you get caught." Stop there. The legal argument is usually better than the "it's not good for you" argument. He knows you're concerned, and I think he'll be glad to hear you say so. I have a feeling that all his lies are just a means of bringing out that concern.

# VII

## Recklessness

Nothing gets a parent more uptight than worrying about a child who is careless, foolhardy, and in general shows too little regard for his or her safety. Unfortunately, you can rarely correct the situation by imploring the youngster to "be careful." Such pleas or demands often touch off even more recalcitrance, making a parent's life still more unbearable. This is when mama really begins to wish that her child was a tractable little dumpling like the placid kid next door.

Well, when I was a child, I wasn't placid, but I was tractable as hell. Whatever my mama or daddy told me to do, I did. And what was the result? They were spared the pain of worry and anxiety, but I was always in a bind because I had to live with so much frustration. By not giving them any trouble, I gave myself trouble. When I reached adolescence, I found myself unable to stick to my studies, make decisions about my life, or untangle my mixed-up feelings. I wanted to do something really reckless, like committing suicide. Lucky for me, I had some very understanding teachers and maybe some intuitive feel for looking into myself that helped me overcome my hangups.

Why do I mention all this?

Because I'd like to reassure parents that reckless children may be better off when they. mature than kids who've gone out of their way to spare their parents anxiety and worry. Of course, these children have to be restrained from going too far and destroying themselves. That's where the problem is tougher on the parent than on the child. That's when you hear a mother or father complain, "I've tried everything and nothing works!"

Well, there are some things that can be made to work to relieve parental anxiety and to make kids sufficiently tractable to keep them from endangering themselves. It often boils down to a matter of whose will is going to prevail: the parent's or the child's. Strong-willed kids are no picnic. However, the object shouldn't be to destroy that will but to harness all that stubborn energy so it can be used more constructively.

When the family situation gets out of hand and results in a battle of wills, parents sometimes "win" only by destroying the child's will. That is no win. In this chapter, I hope to demonstrate how winning can be enjoyed by both sides and not as the product of a contest that leaves one—parent or child—powerless and broken.

*How do you warn a careless child to be careful of muggers when coming home alone from school, or at night, without turning him into a namby-pamby or a scaredy-cat?*

Don't think in terms of "warning"; think in terms of "informing" the child. The way in which that information is handled is what influences a child to be anxious or simply cautious. Kids, especially careless ones, have to be made aware of potential dangers and taught to take sensible precautions. Also, parents have to offset the panic potential of sensational headlines and television newscasts. If your neighborhood has a serious crime problem, your youngster should be told to avoid trouble by walking with other kids, staying on the curb side, and choosing streets at night that are well-illuminated. If you can't tell him these things without revealing your own fears, have the other parent do so, or call upon an older brother or sister, someone who won't feel as emotional about it. The right time to bring it up is when something has happened in the neighborhood. For example, I knew a family whose home was burglarized. Their eleven-year-old daughter walked in after the burglars had gone, saw the place was a mess, and became terrified. Rooted to the spot, she screamed hysterically, finally attracting the attention of a neighbor who rushed in and comforted her until her parents returned. Now, if I lived in that neighborhood, I would mention to my child that a nearby house had been burglarized and some things were taken, but nobody was hurt. It would give me an excuse to remind my child to ring the doorbell—even if she has a key—when she comes home, just in case a burglar might still be inside and thus to give him a chance to get away through the back door. By alerting my child this way, I'd feel she'd know what to expect and would never panic like that other little girl.

*Is there some foolproof method to stop a little daredevil from running away from home?*

I don't know any foolproof methods to stop a child from doing anything. What doesn't work for you may work for somebody else; what doesn't work for one child may work for another; what doesn't work today may work tomorrow. I'll give you some good techniques that can work, but you may have to vary them to make them effective for you and your child. This is especially so for the child who runs away or threatens to run away. You're dealing here with an act of defiance. If you become too authoritative, he'll defy you more; so you have to bend a little. When you sense he's going to run away, say quite unexpectedly, "How would you like to go across town to visit grandma?" Or send him on an errand to the next town. Tell him how late the buses run, but don't lay down the law on when he should be back home. You're inviting him to run, you see, but within limits. You're sending him to places he's never visited alone before and trusting him to take care of himself. There's a calculated risk in this approach, I know, but it's preferable to letting him go off by himself God-knows-where. If the child is very young—six or seven, say—the child's own insecurity may set limits so that you might call his bluff and say, "Okay, go ahead and run." I met a mother who did just that. Her little boy slammed out of the house and she was worried sick. A few minutes later, the boy returned and said angrily, "I'm back! You know I can't cross the street by myself!" You have to handle each runaway threat one at a time, coming up with one temporary solution after another until the child gives up the need to run.

*When nobody—including the family doctor and a psychotherapist—has been able to get a twelve-year-old to quit smoking pot, what is the next step?*

You've been through everybody's front door without success; now try going through the back door. Kids like this are often unreachable by doctors, "straight" friends, or family members. Aside from any potential harm to the child, there is always the possibility that the rest of the family will look down on him because he smokes. His older siblings may not want him to stop because as long as he continues, they feel superior. His younger siblings, however, may want to smoke, too, so they can be like their big brother. And the parents' emotions might be a mix of concern, shame, and anger. This is why help may have to come from outside. All right, then, what do I mean by the "back door"? I mean going out of your way to locate other parents whose kids smoked, or popped pills, or took shots, and who quit. Why did they quit? This is something neither you nor I can tell your child. Only the kids who quit can do this. They learned from experience and are proud of themselves for having quit. Their plain talk can be more convincing to your child than a parent's "no-no" or formal "treatment." If I were you, I'd seek out the parents of such kids and discuss the problem with them. Meanwhile, you should certainly indicate your disapproval of smoking, but avoid arguments with the child. He could be just experimenting. The more pressure you put on him, the more he'll rebel against your authority or anybody else's, which is what he's been doing. He might even go on to "hard stuff" like heroin or opiates. Try the "back door."

## RECKLESSNESS

*If a child is reckless with his allowance—giving it away, treating his friends, always a soft touch—what can you do to keep him from being a patsy?*

The first step is to be sure you aren't a patsy yourself. Usually one or both parents contribute to this problem because they are soft touches themselves. The youngster is given a generous allowance, goes through it quickly, then somebody feels sorry for him because he's broke and throws him an extra quarter. This practice won't help the child develop a money sense. If you or your partner are such parents, I suggest you resist the impulse to toss the youngster an extra coin or dollar when he's out of spending money. On the other hand, I don't suggest cutting the child's allowance as a means to make him spend more carefully. This would be punitive, and I see no reason to punish this child for being overly generous. Obviously, he's using money to win favor with his companions, who are taking advantage of his generosity. But I wouldn't point this out. If he doesn't know this himself, it's better that he learns the hard way even though it hurts. The best solution is to let the child experience self-deprivation, to be in a spot where he needs a dime and doesn't have it. Then you say, "I'm sorry, son, I already gave you your allowance. If you spent it all, you'll have to wait until next week for your next allowance." And don't relent even if that little "big spender" puts on a long face. He has to learn to take the consequences for his actions. Don't bail him out. If he has too hard a time of it, you might then try breaking his weekly allowance down to a daily allowance. But I'd recommend this measure only as a last resort because such daily doling out and such close supervision could invite rebellion.

*Because this boy is called a "sissy," a "goody-goody," and a "mama's boy," he never refuses a dare and takes some awful chances. What's the solution?*

The solution lies in understanding why the boy is overcompensating to a degree where he is taking unnecessary risks. He feels he has no other choice, you see, if he wants to be respected by his peers. Apparently, he wants such respect very much. I know what this feeling is like because I was taunted as a "mama's boy" myself as a child. I was also a "daddy's boy," being overprotected by both parents. When I got into a scrap to command respect among my friends, I lost even when I won. By this, I mean that every time my daddy learned that I'd been fighting, he punished me. He didn't care if I'd come out the winner or had taken a licking; he just didn't want me fighting because "young gentlemen don't fight." Well, a strange thing happened. The more I fought, the more fearful my parents became and the more they tried to protect me. This is what you have to guard against as a parent. You might think to yourself, "Now, if my son would only be a bit bolder, nobody would taunt him, and he wouldn't have to keep proving himself by taking a dare." This thinking makes sense—but the only way to make him *feel* bolder, and not like a "mama's boy," is for you to be bolder yourself. You must break away from this boy more to give him a chance to feel independent of you. If you're accustomed to cautioning him: "Wear your rubbers," "Put on a heavier sweater, you'll be cold," "Don't do this, don't do that, you might get hurt," make yourself stop. He'll survive. So will you, and you'll feel relieved not to have to worry about him any more.

*How can a small child be stopped from playing with matches and knives? He's making me a nervous wreck!*

I don't know what techniques you've already tried, but if one of them's been to nag at him to stop, that's a good way to become a nervous wreck. It's also likely to be futile. The way kids' minds work, the more you nag at them not to do something, the more they'll do it. The best strategy is simply to take away the matches and knives the first time you see him playing with them. "I need these," is all you have to say, with no explanations or "no-no's" offered. The child could lose interest in such playthings right then and there. Maybe you tried this and it didn't work. All right, by now he knows that matches and knives are taboo. That's too bad because this taboo tends to become more important in the child's mind than the fact that matches and knives are useful tools—when handled properly. A parent can tell a child that he might burn or cut himself, but kids don't truly comprehend what "burn" and "cut" means until they find out for themselves. You have to take a calculated risk. Encourage the child to use matches and knives for a good purpose. Say to him, "Here, come light the oven for me" and "Take this steak knife and cut your own meat." Supervise, watch him, and don't panic if he burns or cuts himself. There's very little chance that such injuries will be more than minor. Patch up any wounds as painlessly and casually as you can. The important thing is that the youngster will be learning, with parental approval, how to use matches and knives as practical tools, not as playthings.

*What do you do with an accident-prone little girl who never watches where she's going, keeps tripping over herself, and alway bangs herself up?*

You have to make sure that she is all right physically. If her eyesight, hearing, or physical coordination is bad, this could be the reason why she's accident-prone. Don't take all these things for granted. Have your doctor check her out. If her problem appears to be purely emotional, store up a lot of patience. This isn't something you cure overnight if you ever cure it at all. What you must try to do is minimize and control the accident-proneness so that the child will avoid any major calamities. Your object over a period of time is to enable the child to establish sufficient self-control without any attention from you. Right now, though, she needs your attention. In fact, her accident-proneness may be her unconscious means of putting subtle pressure on you to get your attention. Well, attend to her if she falls or bangs herself up. But don't make a big thing of it, and don't shout, "I told you that you'd hurt yourself if you weren't careful!" Don't use any of those "I told you sos" because this tends to make the accidents seem like punishment to the child for not listening to you. Don't consider these as acts of disobedience. Such thinking will only make you angry and won't allow you to help the child or yourself. And don't go in the opposite direction and sympathize with her too much. You can't treat accident-proneness with extreme responses. The key is to be casual. Take notice, but not too much, and not too little. Just say, "Are you okay?" When reassured that she is, go about your business. As to her general behavior, show a little more approval than is customary. It will help her self-esteem and reduce any need she has to punish herself.

*Would you believe that a child of twelve would insist on driving his father's car, and has in fact done so several times! How can you stop him?*

You just say "No" the first time he "insists." Spell it out for him so that he understands that you mean what you say: "No . . . N - O . . . No!" If he keeps badgering you to give him reasons, tell him he can't drive the car because it isn't legal for him to do so at his age. If he comes back at you with that overwhelming kind of logic that only kids are capable of, demanding, "What's the difference how old I am as long as I know how to drive? And I know how, better than most drivers!" then you come right back, "Fine, but until they change the law, you can't drive. And that's that." What I'm wondering about, though, is how this young fellow learned to drive at such a young age. Who taught him? Did daddy or an uncle or an adult friend teach him "just for fun"? Or did he learn behind your back, or maybe pick it up just from watching others at the wheel, then trying it himself? Some kids are very skillful mechanically and have remarkable coordination. If such a child is in the regular company of someone who's preoccupied with automobiles, he might very well find himself unable to resist the temptation to try out the car himself. That's why a parent should not teach a small child how to drive "just for fun," then expect him to wait for years until he can experience the thrill himself. But kids, no matter how capable mechanically, lack a sufficient sense of danger to drive safely. He shouldn't be given the wheel even with an adult in the car. What you must do now is transfer his urge to drive from the car to a go-cart or motorized bike, if he persists in wanting to drive. And don't leave the car keys lying around.

*How do you discourage a child from doing foolhardy things like climbing to the top of a tree and threatening to jump. . . . Do you call his bluff and tell him to jump?*

You don't know if he's only bluffing. Maybe he really means to jump. Or maybe he doesn't want to jump but merely wants to worry you and hear you say, "No, no, don't jump!" If you tell him the opposite, "Go ahead and jump!" he might just do so out of spite or to save face. This is a situation where you have to be very, very careful. Better to be overcautious than undercautious. I have worked with kids who put themselves and me in similar situations. I did tell some of them to jump. But I knew these kids very well and could distinguish those who were just grandstanding from those who meant to do away with themselves. It's difficult for a parent to exercise such judgment with certainty because the parent can't always be sufficiently objective. This threat to jump off the top of a tree could be the culmination of a highly emotional disagreement between parent and child. Motivated more by rage than reason, the overwrought parent could easily snap, "Go ahead and jump, you little fool!" You just can't take this chance. It's better to coax him on down quietly and tell him to go to his room until he cools off. Some kids who threaten suicide don't want to carry out that threat, but having gone that far they're ashamed to turn back. When a child reaches this stage of foolhardiness, your decision can be the difference between life and death. As an outsider, I'm not involved with your child's emotions so I can't tell you what to do. I can only tell you what not to do. Don't egg him on to jump. But it's risky for you to handle this alone indefinitely. Bring a psychiatrist or psychologist into the picture.

*Will an eight-year-old who'll try anything—from smoking cigars to hitching rides on the back of a bus—outgrow this desire to show off?*

Not unless you intervene. If you don't, this behavior will snowball and become an integral part of his personality. This showing off does not express a *desire* so much as a *need*. When he shows off, he's trying to tell everyone that he wants to succeed, and to succeed in a big way, to be important. He's probably had a difficult time proving himself capable of success so he's resorted to doing something spectacular to attract notice. He *needs* to succeed to feel like somebody; this is the thing to remember. Now, you can thwart a desire, but you must give him opportunities to satisfy a need. Develop a program for this youngster that will help him to achieve success without having to reach for the spectacular. If he succeeds in doing a lot of little things—and the whole family recognizes such success—the child won't have to attempt one big thing to prove himself. Start out with the premise that this child has a need to feel like a big shot. All right, what are his interests? Use his interests to dream up substitute tasks and goals for which he is suited. Suppose, for example, that he likes geography and travel. Get him some road maps and bus schedules. Ask him if he could map out a bus trip around the country for you. Don't order him to do it; ask him. I think he'll be flattered enough to want to try. Help him if he asks you to, and compliment his efforts. Take his marked-up maps, paste them on a board, and display them proudly right in your living room. This will signify success to him and, I think, serve as a substitute for hitching bus rides. After a few such achievements, I think you'll find he will outgrow his need to show off.

# VIII
## Sexual Peculiarities

It isn't easy to own up to oneself—let alone to somebody else—that one's child is a sexual oddball. It becomes easier, though, when parents begin to realize that the unusual may be more ordinary than they suspected. You see, mamas and daddies tend to become anxious when their child fails to meet their standards of normal sex behavior. Their peace of mind depends on the child's conforming to their ideas of right and wrong. That's fine. But it is equally important—for the child's peace of mind and general mental health—that the parents' judgments be appropriate to that particular child's needs.

Daddy, for example, may turn red with embarrassment if his little girl of six peels off her bathing suit at the beach and jumps into the water naked. Now, this may be a perfectly innocent thing for this little girl to do, but daddy may consider it indecent and paddle her. He means well and is giving her a lesson in decorum that she'll never forget. However, there are better ways to educate a child socially.

Or take another example. Mama walks into her little boy's room and finds him playing with himself. "That's disgusting!" she thinks to herself and slaps the child's hand. She too means well and is also giving a lesson the child will never forget. But this is a lesson that should never be taught this way, if at all. In both examples, other parents might see nothing wrong in either kind of behavior. For them, that little girl would have to go much farther, perhaps taking off her clothes at the supermarket, and that little boy would have to do something much more far-out, perhaps to the point of masturbating in mama's nightie.

Their standards would be more liberal, perhaps too liberal, so that their kids' sex behavior would have to be really oddball before they'd take notice.

Well, when should a parent feel ashamed? When should a sex quirk be overlooked? How do you draw the line between letting a kid go too far, and not letting him go far enough?

The answers to these and similar questions depend on three factors: 1) The degree of "oddball" sex behavior that parents can tolerate comfortably, 2) the child's level of emotional stability as determined by age, feelings in general, and evidence of innocence or sophistication, and 3) the social attitudes of the community. By and large, a child's social maturity—which is measured by the demands of the society in which the youngster is raised—is relative to the child's sexual maturity. This is why, in the long run, the sexual oddball may be doomed to be a loser, a social outcast. And this is why parents have to know how—and when—to cope with sex behavior frowned upon by friends and neighbors.

As a parent, you have to be able to handle your child's sexual curiosity even when it takes bizarre forms, but you must do this without interfering with the youngster's sexual development. I hope that this chapter will help you determine when to correct, instruct, smack, or look the other way.

*Isn't there any way to make a fourth-grader stop masturbating in front of his family, in company, and even in the classroom? Nothing seems to work!*

Something will work. You have to keep trying different techniques. A boy who masturbates in public probably shocks everybody into screaming at him, "Stop that!" I recommend that the next time you see him masturbate openly, you just go over to him and tell him—*privately*—"If you want to do that, please do it in the bathroom." By handling the situation this way, you aren't telling the child that masturbation is bad, dangerous, or freaky, only that it isn't acceptable socially. You control his behavior by encouraging him to use *self*-control—not to stop playing with himself, but only to stop doing so in public. I think you should discourage other members of the family from saying anything to him because they're apt to chastise him. Besides, it's better if only one person assumes the responsibility of re-educating the boy. So tell everybody to lay off the boy, just to bring their complaints to you, and let you handle the situation. If you can't be around at such times, you might instruct them to speak to the child *exactly as you do*. As for his masturbating in class, you'll have to confer with the teacher. Ask her to please ignore the situation until after class is over, then to speak to the child privately about going to the bathroom the next time he wants to play with himself. I've used this technique many times in my classes and found that, eventually, the masturbators did excuse themselves to go to the bathroom. Then, after a while, it became too much bother and so they gave up masturbating during school hours altogether. Even kids get tired of too much of a good thing, you see.

*Is it normal for a small boy to strut about in his sister's clothes?*

If he's five or six, I'd consider it normal; if he's in his teens, I wouldn't; if he's somewhere in between, I wouldn't be sure. Little boys who like to try on mama's high heels and play with dolls are nothing to worry about. They're simply being curious. But if they persist and take special joy in this kind of behavior, you can assume that it's past the point of being regarded as mere curiosity. What is interesting here is that this child dresses up in his *sister's* clothes. Maybe he wants to be like his sister because she is smarter than he is, or maybe more popular, or maybe because she gets more attention at home. Consider those possibilities. If they make sense, take a different attitude to this child, and make him the focus of parental pride and attention. Don't pay notice to his strutting around; find other things to occupy you. Above all, don't taunt him for it and don't giggle over it. Either such reaction will only reinforce his feeling for that kind of behavior and he'll strut all the more. Instead, make the same kind of fuss over how handsome he looks in his own clothes as you would over how pretty his sister looks when she dresses up. This is the old-fashioned technique known as "accentuating the positive." It still works. Try it and see.

*What is wrong with a girl who goes to her room and abuses herself sexually every time she's reprimanded? She's entering junior high school!*

She must be a very sensitive child who becomes terribly anxious when reprimanded. Masturbating comforts her and eases her anxieties. But it's interesting that you don't say "she masturbates"; you say "she abuses herself." I get the feeling that you are altogether too worried about the effects of her playing with herself. Rest assured that the masturbation isn't going to hurt her. What isn't so healthy is the apparent extent of her anxieties and her need to masturbate as a pacifier. I suggest that first of all you stop looking at masturbation as "self-abuse." Then I think you should become aware that your daughter is more sensitive, more feeling, than most girls her age. Obviously, she can't cope with a scolding. Maybe she needs a little more freedom to make mistakes without being corrected? When she does require reprimanding, do it as gently as possible to avoid arousing fear. Perhaps someone else should do the reprimanding. If daddy's in charge now, the mama should take over, and vice versa. This child seems to need to be tended like a flower and nurtured slowly, gently, patiently. She is a rare human being and will reward your patience by blossoming into a more self-assured young woman of great kindness and consideration.

*How do you answer a ten-year-old's vulgar questions that suggest an obsessive interest in sex?*

I'd answer as directly as I could without going into a lot of detail. A boy that age once asked me, "Monty, what's a cocksucker?" He sure as hell took me by surprise! Well, I just shrugged my shoulders and said, "A cock is a slangy word for penis; that's what all boys urinate with. And cocksucker is another slangy word that some foolish kids use to insult people they don't like. It's like calling someone a shitass. Now, that doesn't mean the kid has shit on his ass, and being called a cocksucker doesn't mean the kid sucks on his penis. It's just a slobby kind of insult, you see, and people will think you're a slobby kind of kid if you go around using it." That's pretty rough talk, but it's the kind of talk this child wanted and could comprehend. I leveled with him so that he'd continue to trust me with his questions, but I let him know that he was using language that would turn people off. You have to remember that most kids are "obsessed" not with sex but with "dirty" words. They compensate for their embarrassment by using vulgarity. Now this can be pretty offensive to a parent accustomed to modesty. But I always say to such a parent: "Isn't it better that your child asks *you* rather than some kid who might mislead him?" Don't you be embarrassed. You know what the words mean. Take your time before answering, cool down, then answer as biologically as the child can comprehend. Don't give fuzzy answers or the child will get a distorted view of sex. Take the mystery out of the "dirty" words and "vulgar" questions by tackling them directly and reducing them to pure biology. It'll be a load off your mind, and off his.

*If an eleven-year-old girl gives many indications of having lesbian tendencies—wears her hair like a boy's, is a real tomboy, competes with boys in sports—should she be sent to an all-girl summer camp?*

You don't cure homosexuality by sending a child away to camp, or to boarding school. If you do decide to send her, select a co-ed camp, and be sure that there will be at least two other girls in her room. The third girl will serve as a preventive in case there is any attempt to act out sexually. Also, I wouldn't pass on my suspicions to the camp director, if I were you. The child would be watched like a hawk and be distrusted, if she were admitted in the first place. But I'm wondering if you aren't reading too much into this girl's "boyishness" altogether. It makes sense to keep an eye on her, but it could be dangerous to jump to hasty conclusions. Treat her like a girl—not like a girl who is acting like a boy—without suggesting that she isn't behaving femininely enough to suit your taste. Buy her girlish things to wear but don't press her to wear flouncy "feminine" clothes. Encourage her to help you around the house—especially with cooking and baking—and take her along with you on shopping trips more often. I am not saying that your fears are unfounded. I am saying that the youngster is still at an age when you can be mistaken in your observations. In such situations, I prefer to give the child the benefit of the doubt while making available to her more opportunities to feel secure about her femininity.

*Should you chastise a small boy for taking his mother's underclothes into bed with him?*

I wouldn't chastise him. I'd just say, "Those are mine," and take them away. I'd treat it no differently than his daddy would if the boy had grabbed his pajamas. "Hey, son, those are my pajamas," daddy would say. "Give them back, you've got your own." The idea is to take the sexual significance out of the child's behavior. I'd also take stock of how underclothes are treated generally in the household. Does mama hide her bra when she takes it off? Does she hide herself when she's in her nightgown? Is she ashamed to dry her stockings over the bathtub? Remember, these garments used to be called "unmentionables," and in some families they still are treated so. I know mothers who are too embarrassed even to hang their under things out on the clothesline. Well, there's nothing wrong with being modest, but too much modesty is usually a cover-up for feelings of shame. Kids can see through this kind of cover. This may not be the case at all in your home. Still, if I were you, I'd go out of my way to be calculatingly casual about "unmentionables." Let the boy take his parents' underclothes along with his own and his brothers' and sisters' down to the washing machine or the laundromat. Let him hang them out on the clothesline to dry. There's nothing abnormal about a boy hanging his mama's, or his sister's, panties on the clothesline—if it's treated as an ordinary household chore. Don't make a big deal of it. Be casual. Then, instead of underthings being viewed as sexy, they'll be viewed as commonplace. Unless you do this now, the youngster's behavior could be symptomatic of trouble to come in the future.

*Isn't a boy of seven old enough to know he should stand up to urinate, and not sit on the toilet?*

He was old enough years ago. But has he had any opportunities to learn? All the boys I've met who sat on the pot to pee instead of standing up were kids who'd never once been to the bathroom with their daddies. This is one of the natural functions that isn't taught verbally. You don't say to a boy, "Stand up when you urinate," or to a girl, "Sit down." This is something that is taught by example. It's generally handled unconsciously by the parents. When very young, a boy finds himself sharing the bathroom quite naturally with daddy, a girl with her mama. As a result, there is no sexual confusion. However, it is mama who has the job of introducing small children— of both sexes—to the bathroom. She can't set an example for her son. What she can do is stand him up against the pot, help him to open his fly, and direct him to urinate. But she can only do this when he is big enough to reach the toilet. She might lift him up if he isn't, but she is more likely to let him just sit down instead. Unless the child accompanies an older boy or a man to the bathroom, he becomes used to sitting down. It is high time for this boy's daddy to share the bathroom with his son. He needn't tell the youngster to stand up. All he has to do is set an example. His son will copy him. If he doesn't do so at once, nothing should be said. Above all, the child should not be ridiculed. After a few such experiences, I'm pretty sure the boy will copy daddy's urinating style. If I were daddy, I'd also let the child keep me company when I shaved or showered. I'd buy him a toy razor, let him squirt some shaving cream on his face and "shave" with me. This is how I'd go about repatterning his behavior in masculine terms.

*Is there something peculiar about a twelve-year-old girl's interest in staring at her nude image in a full-length mirror?*

Well, it's not the usual way for a child to look at herself. If this is a regular habit, I'd be concerned. It could be a sign that she's having difficulty with sexual identification, that she's uncertain of her femininity or dissatisfied with it. Try to help her think more of herself, especially of her body. If she has a nice little figure, tell her so. If she's on the heavy side, help her lose some weight without being too obvious about it. Feed her dishes that are tasty, pretty to look at, but not fattening. This will put you to a lot of trouble, I know, but I think you'll find satisfaction in her look of pleasure when she sees herself slimmer in the mirror. It would be a good idea also to take more interest in her clothes. Let her accompany you to the store and select with you clothes that she likes. This will bring attention to her physical attractiveness. Sometimes a little girl who stares at herself this way is competing with her mama, especially if mama is pretty and has a nice figure. One such girl said to me, "I wish I could be like my mother so daddy would look at me the way he does her." Well, this mama was a very sexy-looking gal who dressed to make the most of her well-developed figure. She toned down the sexiness and her husband toned down his extreme admiration and the outspoken remarks that went with it. Both parents turned more attention on to the child until she no longer felt like mama's rival. I've found that kids who stare at their nude images for long periods sometimes reinforce their dissatisfaction with what they see to a point where they become self-destructive. You can head this off, not by nagging, but by helping the child feel more adequate as a female.

*What can you do about a boy who keeps having erections in class and is ashamed to get up and recite?*

Well, there's a bare chance that it could be a urological problem—like having an erection upon awakening that disappears after urinating—so I'd have my family doctor check the boy out physically. But I think it more likely that the youngster is beginning to feel his sexuality and is full of young juice. In most situations I've come across, I've found that these kids are wearing shorts and pants that are too tight. They rub against his penis. Since he's emotionally and biologically ripe for such stimulation, his penis grows hard and there's very little he can do about it except concentrate more on his studies in order to block out his emotions. If he complains to you of being embarrassed in class, suggest that he concentrate more on his lesson by keeping his eyes glued to his book. More important, however, is for you to see that he wears loose clothing. If he's wearing jockey shorts, switch him to boxer shorts. Have him wear slacks that are looser in the crotch. If his teacher is an understanding human being, you might talk to him, or her, privately without your son's knowledge. Explain frankly that the boy is going through a developmental stage that sometimes makes it embarrassing for him to stand up to recite. It's possible that the boy is masturbating so much at home that he's conditioning his penis to behave the wrong way at the wrong time. Don't stop him. But try to get him more interested in athletics, exercise, and active hobbies to drain off some of his juices in a nonsexual way. Try getting him to bathe in the morning, before going to school, instead of the night before. Such baths could have a soothing, calming influence. Encourage him to have lots of friends to keep him from being alone too much in order to reduce his opportunities for sexual fantasizing. And relax; the problem's only temporary.

*If a child is definitely homosexual, is there any hope for change?*

That depends on the child. If he's hell-bent on being a homosexual, he's going to remain a homosexual. Now this is an awful burden for a parent to bear, but you have to learn to live with it. Don't blame yourself. Nobody knows for sure if homosexuality is a product of biochemistry or social chemistry. But don't jump to hasty conclusions, and don't misread so-called "signs" of homosexuality. Is the boy really engaging in sex with another boy? Is he revolted by girls, or simply shy? Who says he's a homosexual—your friends, your doctor, he himself, you? If there's the slightest doubt, and if the boy gives evidence that he doesn't want to be homosexual, then you can help him change. His daddy should give him more, not less, affection and attention. And his mama must be careful not to try to seduce him into liking girls, for this kind of tactic will have the reverse effect. But if you're convinced that his inclinations are definitely homosexual, don't reject the child. Instead, teach him—just as you would about ordinary sex relations—the dangers of promiscuity and venereal disease. Teach him the rules of social behavior, the need for mutual consent in sexual relationships. Don't do these things now, but prepare yourself now for the need to do them later when the child grows older. Please understand that I'm not waving the flag for homosexuality. This is a heterosexual world that is tough on those who go a different route. I'd make this plain to the boy if he were my son. But my goal, like yours, would be his future happiness. He might function better, in work and in love, as a homosexual than he would if he pretended to be what he isn't. You must constantly keep this in mind to give you strength enough to cope. All I've said pertains as well to would-be lesbians.

# IX

# Destroying

The destructive child is likely to be punished *too* severely or else to be so feared that all discipline breaks down and the child is out of parental control. Both extremes fail to provide the child with what he needs and is actually asking for: an evenhanded kind of discipline that will lead to self-control. Until the child learns self-control, life can be hell for the whole family.

Well, just how destructive must a child be before parents clamp down? What kind of clamping down is called for: A smack? A scolding? The forfeit of some treat? Should a girl be treated the same as a boy? These are some aspects of the problem that this chapter will deal with.

It's self-evident that the child who destroys things, or who lashes out at other kids (or adults) is a very angry youngster. What isn't self-evident is the reason for such anger. Some say, "Oh, he was born mad at the world." Well, I don't think anyone is born mad at the world. It's possible, though, that he was born with a more delicate nervous system than most kids and so might be more susceptible to little angers that others could shrug off. Then there are those who say, "Oh, it's just that he wasn't brought up right even though his parents seem to be good people." Well, there may be something to that, too, but even the best parents can't always be as perfect as they might like to be. Parents, too, are human. They may try their best but life often deals with them harshly. They may be preoccupied with earning a living, or taking care of sick relatives, or ministering to a marriage that isn't all they'd hoped for. Sidetracked by such distractions, they may not become fully aware of their child's relative inability to cope with frustration, hurt feelings, or deep-seated animosities. Nevertheless, when destructive tendencies do become apparent, it is not a time for parents to waste their energies in self-blame, guilt, or regrets. It is a time to get down to the business at hand and deal with the situation promptly and confidently.

If you witness an isolated incident—a child breaks something or beats up another kid—a firm "no-no" may be sufficient. There's no need to pile on long lectures and strong punishments. It is enough to make the child understand that what he's done will not be tolerated the second time. He may react with remorse, an apology, or become more belligerent. Just stand firm. Don't undertake lengthy explanations for your feelings. Your indignation is righteous and the put-down is equally righteous.

If the destructive incident is extreme—fire-setting, for example—or repetitive, you have to take stronger measures. In any case, it is appropriate for the entire family to present a united front, to share the sense of indignation; but it is not appropriate for all members of the family to act as disciplinarians. A child cannot and should not be disciplined by his brothers and sisters. This is a job for the parents, and each should back up the other to make such discipline effective. Often, the key to success is to do the unexpected, as this chapter will demonstrate.

*Is there anything you can do with a child who rips off his clothes, button by button, seam by seam, and often in public?*

Well, you can try to find out why he does this. But that's going to take a long time. All you want to do is get him to stop because it's embarrassing to you and bad for the boy socially. Let's look at it that way. Now, this is compulsive behavior, and you can't get such a child to stop by begging or threatening him. It won't penetrate. Here's a little trick I've used effectively with kids like this. You take some of your own clothes—a shirt, a skirt, a pair of pants—and a needle and thread, and go into the child's room. Say to him, "I hope you don't mind my coming in here and sitting on your bed to do some sewing. The light's better here, and I tore my shirt and have to fix it." The youngster will want to watch what you're doing, so show him the rip. Explain how tricky it is to thread the needle and sew, but be sure to show him how much you enjoy doing these things. When you finish the job, take the mended shirt with you and drop the subject. A few days later, repeat the performance with some other article of clothing. Take a few stitches, then get out. Never ask the child if he wants to try using the needle and thread. That has to come from him. After three or four times, you'll find that the child will reach for the needle and thread to try it himself. Don't let him fail. Encourage him. Say to him: "You do that better than I do. That's right, pull the needle through the cloth. Now see how nicely that skinny thread is holding those old pants together?" Then leave the needle with him, and leave all kinds of thread, all colors, and you'll find that he'll be mending, not tearing, his clothes.

*How in heaven's name can you teach a little girl of seven to stop messing up her lovely room? It looks like a pig sty!*

I have a feeling that this little girl just isn't interested in having such a lovely room. Children of both sexes often feel hemmed in by too much neatness, too much "niceness," because in such surroundings they can't be themselves. They have to be careful not to mess up the curtains, the fancy furniture, or the pretty pictures on the wall. When they stop being careful, they're actually saying to their parents: "These nice things please you but they don't mean much to me. I don't want to be fussy and look after them." Now this little seven-year-old might make her mama much happier if her room was homey, but functional, not cluttered, but not barren either. Remove the fripperies. Keep the room simple. The less clutter, the easier the room will be to keep clean and neat, and mama won't be so upset if her little gal messes it up now and then. You see, the main thing here is to reduce the need to be a harsh disciplinarian. You do this by making the room easier to take care of. If you straighten it up when it needs straightening, without the need to feel so upset, you'll become less rigid in your expectations and the child will learn to become neater. She may never learn to place as high a value on prettiness as you do, but that's her privilege and pride enough for her. I've known mothers who went around slapping their kids' hands every time they moved something out of place, saying, "No, you mustn't move the picture, you mustn't crease the bedspread, you mustn't leave your things around like that." Well, that won't teach a child to conform. It'll only make the kid madder than hell and really destructive.

*Should parents stand by and allow their hot-tempered child to cut himself smashing windows in order to teach him a lesson?*

There's no need to let him cut himself. What's important here is not that he be taught a lesson but that he be encouraged to discharge some of that anger so that you and he can start communicating. I've known many kids with low boiling points who went on window-smashing rages. When I thought it would be good for them, I did the unexpected—gave them baseball bats and said, "Go ahead, break all the windows you want." I knew they wouldn't hurt themselves. I also suspected that eventually they'd tire of the sport. Like your child, these kids were hot-tempered and all bottled-up with angry steam that needed to be let off. When they smashed the windows with the baseball bats, that anger steamed off and the kids became accessible to reason. That's when I took the bats away and sat down to talk to them. They thought I was pretty crazy to give them bats and let them break windows. It was totally unexpected, you see, and it gave them a jolt. Now they began to trust me more, and because they trusted me I was able to influence them. It took a lot of broken windows before they became able to voice their feelings instead of acting them out, but it was very inexpensive therapy in the long run. Now, there are other kids who will break windows just out of spite. Well, I didn't give such kids baseball bats. When they broke windows, I knew they were thumbing their noses at me. I told them in no uncertain terms to cut it out, made them pick up the pieces of broken glass (with gloves on), and do chores to earn the cost of replacing the windows. If they refused to do these things, I paddled them. Only the smart aleck, you see, needs to be taught a lesson.

*Every time this child breaks something, throws something, or strikes someone, she says "I'm sorry" and asks to be forgiven, but later on acts up again! What can you do?*

Stop being so forgiving. Kids are smarter than you think. This child is manipulating you. She knows she has you in a bind every time she says "I'm sorry." Furthermore, she may truly believe that her apology automatically undoes the mischief; the more times you forgive, the stronger will grow her belief that just the words "I'm sorry" automatically make things right. So, you see, there's nothing to deter her from doing more mischief. Something else happens, too. The child learns to associate feeling sorry with doing something wrong. This means that if *you* should ever say "I'm sorry," maybe because you forgot her birthday present or were late in meeting her after school—any perfectly legitimate oversight—then she will automatically think that *you* did something wrong. She won't be able to distinguish a reasonable social oversight from malicious mischief. Therefore, it's very important that you break this chain of automatic thinking and instant forgiveness. Don't be hesitant to correct your child. I know fathers who tell their wives, "Give the kid his way. If you get him angry, he'll only give you a hard time and get all upset." Well, sometimes it's a good thing for a child to get upset. Kids have to learn that they can't misbehave to their hearts' content and then apologize their way out with an "I'm sorry." You have to tell your daughter, "Being sorry is no excuse. Don't do that again." If she does it again, punish her in a way that's most comfortable for you and most effective for the child. Maybe just your tone of voice will be sufficient to let her know that you're displeased. Let her know, and at once.

*If your eight-year-old is the talk of the neighborhood because he scrawls the word "fuck" on people's walks, fences, and walls, how do you deal with him?*

You must first decide what you and the neighbors find most objectionable: his lack of respect for other people's property or the particular word he scrawls on it. This will dictate your approach. If the neighbors are up in arms because their property's being defaced, no matter how—don't pussyfoot around. You have to live with these people, and they have the right to expect you to control your child. Take the chalk away from him, give him a sponge and pail of water, and tell him to clean up his scribblings. At the same time, give him a piece of your own backyard on which he's permitted to scribble away all he wants. By doing this, you help him to understand that he has to respect other people's property but that what he does with his own is his own business. Now, if the neighbors (and you) are more uptight about the word he's scribbling, your strategy has to be pointed to switching him over to more acceptable words. Ask him if he knows what the word "fuck" means. I have a notion he doesn't. But I'll bet he knows it's the kind of word that is taboo, that it will bug people, and that he uses it for that reason. Kids like to get a rise out of grown-ups. However, they know that if they say words like "fuck" out loud, they're likely to be hollered at. So they scrawl it on a wall, like graffiti, in a kind of sneaky one-upmanship. If I were you, I'd make it clear to this youngster that he can use the word among his friends but not in public. Explain that you would rather have him use the word "love," which means almost the same thing. If he doesn't, he'll have to stop marking everything up. I'll bet that will take all the fun out of it for him and he'll stop scribbling altogether.

*Is a boy's father right when he insists that it will do a little troublemaker good to be sent away for discipline?*

He couldn't be more wrong! Where does he want him sent away? To a military school? A reform school? Either choice is wrong. This is an old-fashioned kind of disciplinary attitude that assumes a youngster will be "straightened out" by rigid drill-sergeant techniques. Some parents encourage their kids to join the Army, Navy, or Marines for this purpose. It rarely works. When it does, it's not because the youngster was a troublemaker so much as that he simply needed a more highly structured environment. I have a feeling that this boy's daddy is at his wit's end, has given up, and wants somebody else to take over the job of teaching the boy to have more self-control. I'd like to encourage him to take another stab at it himself. In my experience, I've found that when a child gets out of hand, his daddy either lets the reins go altogether and becomes too tolerant or else clamps down too hard and tries to beat or bully the child into submission. Either response is perfectly understandable, but both are equally ineffective. I'd set a firm, even stern, course of action to bring this boy in line, without raising my voice and without wavering from any decision I'd made. I'd also make sure that mama backed me up all the way so that the boy couldn't turn one parent against the other to his own advantage. If my emotions had got me past the point where I could do this, I would arrange to have a few sessions of psychotherapy for myself—not for the boy—so that I could regain sufficient emotional stability to deal with the problem firmly, sternly, and effectively. By talking out my feelings with an understanding person, I would become more understanding myself. It would be cheaper than military school and better for my own emotional health.

*This little girl threatens destruction to everyone including herself (she once threatened to hang herself as a "joke"), but doesn't act on her threats. Is she sick?*

Well, "sick" is a big word that is often used as a label to stick on anyone who behaves differently from most people. Don't think of her as sick but as troubled. Usually, you don't have to worry too much about the kid who threatens. She's expressing her feelings. I'm not afraid of the one who talks things out. I am afraid of the one who's quiet. If she were merely threatening destruction to others, I'd be inclined to call her bluff—so long as I could be around to keep an eye on her. I'd say, "You want to hit your big sister? Go ahead. But don't complain if she hits you back." Most kids who threaten will back down. But here you have a complication. This girl has threatened to hang herself as a "joke." Well, you can't treat it as a joke. She may be all bluster, but you can't take that chance. You have to regard this threat as a matter of life and death, and you must tell her so. "Death is final," say to her. "There's no coming back to life again, and don't you forget it." It's better to make her frightened of dying than frightened of living. Too many kids these days *are* attempting suicide, and many such attempts are preceded by what were regarded as empty threats. You have to put the fear of death in her. But you aren't going to stop feeling anxious until she stops using such threats. I'm pretty sure she's using them to get attention. Well, instead of paying attention to the threats, give her more attention when she *doesn't* threaten anyone. Also, give her a chance to unload her anger and frustration. Let daddy say to her, "Honey, if you want to hit somebody, hit me." I've used that technique many times, taking their pummeling to let them get the hostility out of their systems. It works.

*How do you stop a child from being a bully?*

The best way is to find another bully who will knock the daylights out of the youngster without hurting him, just hit him hard enough to make him think twice the next time he wants to bully anybody. I admit that this is a primitive way of dealing with the problem, but sometimes primitive methods work best.

However, you have to be artful to make this primitive approach possible. You see, you're ashamed that your child is a bully, but you can't help him directly, only indirectly. You can't beat him up. You have to manipulate matters so that one of his peers will do it. You tell your child, "If you keep up your bullying, one of these days you're going to get the shit knocked out of you. And don't tell me I didn't warn you." Feel free to talk to him this way because this is the language a bully understands. Remember, this doesn't mean you love your child the less. It means you're trying to help him get along better in society, and you must begin now when his character is still plastic. Naturally, you have to guard against his being hurt to the point of getting his nose broken or his teeth knocked out. He needs only a good pounding to put him on notice that some of his victims will fight back. The easiest way to manage this is to tell the parent who complains that your son has hit her son, "Make him hit him back." If it's the child who complains, say, "You're as strong as he is. Don't be afraid to tangle with him. Hit him back the next time he picks on you." But make it clear that this is not to be a grudge fight that goes on and on. It stops right here once the other kid gets in his licks. So don't give your approval to the kind of kid who, once he gets a taste of blood, will want more. That will turn it into a vendetta. Just get the other kid to hit back. This is one case where your boy has to learn from his peers, not from you, but with your subtle help.

*What's the best way to handle a mischievous little boy who torments pets, starts fires, and plays other such pranks?*

Try to turn the tables on him. These pranks are foolish, cruel, and potentially dangerous. I'm sure you've tried reasoning, pleading, and maybe even thrashings, and nothing has succeeded. All right, now try to reach him by playing some harmless "pranks" on him that will surprise him, make him temporarily unhappy and drive home a point. Say, for example, that he's tied a tin can to the dog's tail. Now, he expects to be bawled out, perhaps spanked. Well, don't punish him or scold him. Just pick up the dog and say, "Now I'm going to play a prank on you because you were cruel to your pet. I'm taking away your dog and giving him to someone who'll be nicer to him. When you stop playing such pranks, I might surprise you again by letting you have him back." If he starts a fire in the backyard or the living room, just put it out and stay calm. Don't stick his hand in the flame to "teach him a lesson." Say to him, "You know you shouldn't do that. Now I have a surprise for you. We're all going to the amusement park tomorrow and you're going to stay home!" If he says to you, "But I didn't mean it, mom," then give him another chance, but tell him, "Don't do it again." Keep in mind that there's a big difference between the child who owns up to his mischief and one who denies any wrongdoing. If the child owns up, you're ahead of the game. The act of confession is good and you should accept the child's apology. But if he does it again and again, you must treat him the same way you would the child who denied it. Turn the prank around by surprising him with an unexpected deprivation. If, after a time, you still haven't made your point, you'll have to accompany the next deprivation with a quick smack to enforce your authority.

*Should a parent forgive a six-year-old who tried to smother his baby sister in her crib?*

This is your son. Who else should forgive him? But you should also reprimand him and make him understand what a dangerous thing he has done. Forgiveness doesn't mean giving him license to behave this way again. It means accepting and trying to understand this child simply because he is your son, just as that innocent little girl is your daughter, and both children merit your protection. Angry as you are, try not to make the boy feel like a monster. Give yourself time for your anger to subside, then say to him, "Son, you just don't do such things. This is your little sister. She needs you to protect her. See how gently mama and daddy treat you. Well, that's how you must treat her." From this point on, you're going to have to be more vigilant. If the boy was unaware of what he had done, you've made him aware. But if he was aware all the time, you have the difficult task now of helping him to overcome his apparent desire or need to hurt the baby. Is he jealous? Does the baby get all the attention of the grandparents and other relatives? Is this boy an especially sensitive child? Sometimes there's a large gap between the ages of the two children. In such cases, the older one often feels quite suddenly deprived of the status he formerly enjoyed and turns against the baby whom he holds responsible. Well, make *him* feel responsible for her well-being. The worst thing to do is warn him, "Don't ever dare touch that baby again!" It will make him furious, more jealous than ever. Instead, enlist his help. Say to him, "Come on, son, you're the big boy here. I'm going to leave baby alone. You watch over her." This makes him her protector and restores the status he has lost. And it corrects a possible tendency to overprotect the baby and overdiscipline the older child.

# X

# Not Making It Intellectually

Today's kids are better educated than their parents. This doesn't mean they're smarter. It only means that they know more than their parents did when they were their age. They're years ahead in sophistication, not because they're more intelligent, but simply because they're better informed. If many kids seem to have more (or less) common sense than your generation and mine, it's only because common sense nowadays is measured by different standards and values than it used to be.

Never has there been so much emphasis placed upon education and the ultimate acquisition of academic degrees. Parents sometimes work up feverishly high expectations for their kids, expectations that are fanned by the teachers and the schools who push the kids to achieve—often beyond their natural ability. When kids exceed their abilities in order to "make it," their drive for learning is thwarted and their emotional life takes a terrible beating. I've known lots of kids, bright as hell, who never shared the expectations of their teachers, their classmates, or their parents. They were bound to fail, and their mamas and daddies died inside a thousand times watching their kids stumble their way to failure.

Now, I'm not proposing that the poor student be encouraged to cop out and work below his potential. On the contrary, I'm convinced that the child who can't work to his full potential is headed for serious trouble. But just what is that potential? To answer that question objectively, you have to understand not only the child, but also yourself and your ambitions for the child.

Emotional problems can severely limit a youngster's capacity to learn. The emotional difficulties have to be resolved before the intellect can function at its fullest potential. In many instances, children with emotional problems are put down as mentally retarded when they aren't retarded at all. On the other hand, the child who is truly retarded—for reasons ranging from brain damage to a hard-to-explain lag in maturational development—is often bothered emotionally because of his inability to keep up with his companions. Such kids are baffled by the learning process, and their unhappy parents are driven into a corner—helpless, disappointed, and, often, ashamed.

I tell you that every child, no matter how retarded, can improve. But they have to be reeducated emotionally, socially, and then intellectually, in that order. You have to create a climate for learning. You may have to whittle down your expectations. A severely brain-damaged child may be able to advance only so far, but he can advance. But most kids labeled as retarded are far from backward in all areas. One such youngster told me with a straight face, "I may be retarded but I'm not stupid!" And you know something? He wasn't stupid, or he wouldn't have had the wit—even the unconscious wit—to make that remark.

I don't like to pin labels on kids. I just say, "Here's a child who can do better." Labels make a mama's hair turn gray, and there's no need for mama to have premature gray hairs. In this chapter, I'm going to deal with the need to size up a child's intellectual potential sensibly and take suitable steps to bring the child up to that potential.

*If your youngster asks you to help him with his homework so he can boost his grades and make the honor class as his friends have, should you give that help?*

I'd help him if he was having trouble understanding the work and needed encouragement. I wouldn't do his work for him. I'd help him interpret the questions, then have him answer as best he can. I'd check it out and try to point out wherever he went wrong. Then I'd have him do the work again and hand it in to his teacher. However, I wouldn't do any helping at all to boost a child into an honor class. If he can't make it on his own, he doesn't belong there. If his friends are intellectual snobs who taunt him for not making it, he's better off without their "friendship." This boy is competing beyond his capacity or ability if he needs your help so desperately. What happens when you can no longer help him because *you* don't understand the work? Or because you're just too busy? Or because he goes away to college and you aren't around? Be glad he asked for your help. It's a signal that he's under too much academic pressure. Encourage him to work with full steam at his own level of competence. He'll do better because he'll feel more comfortable when you instill in the child the joy of learning, not the joy of high grades. If he likes to learn, he'll get good enough grades without anybody's help. Even more important, with his sights lowered, he'll feel less frustrated and have a better chance to succeed in everything he touches. It's the frustrated kids, high marks and all—because the marks are never high enough to suit them—who become disappointed in themselves and look for other outlets: drugs, sex, delinquency, you name it.

*Can a disturbed little girl who is supposedly bright but who babbles incoherently ever learn to speak well and read aloud?*

Sure, but it will take lots of patience on your part. Take the child aside each day at times when she is relatively calm and relaxed. Decide to devote yourself to her exclusively for five to ten minutes (you won't keep her attention much longer). Present your "lessons" as play, and don't be authoritative like a teacher. Get down to the child's level, as a playmate, but be decisive: call the shots, steer her attention to where you want it, exercise authority subtly. Babble with her while showing her familiar objects such as apples, books, or dolls, and pictures of familiar things. You can even hold or rock the child if that makes her (and you) more comfortable. Now, make a little game of the words you want her to learn. But don't start with the words, start with the sounds. Take the word, "ball," for example. From an unintelligible "bluhbluhbluh," begin enunciating the consonant "b." Repeat, repeat, repeat until the child absorbs the sound and repeats it back to you. Do it singsong fashion if it amuses her. Then, playing with the ball, add the vowel sound, and say, "baw baw baw," again repeating until the youngster picks it up. Finally, enunciate the whole word, "ball," repeating it over and over slowly until she sounds it for you. A sound at a time, a word at a time, before you start introducing simple sentences like "Bounce the ball" and so on. If the little girl shows absolutely no interest, postpone the "lesson." After a few weeks, you can lengthen the sessions to the point where her attention starts to waver. It will be a long slow process, but you're going to feel pretty damned excited when your daughter articulates her very first word, be it "ball" or "booze."

*When a nine-year-old is interested only in sports, rock music, and play, and his father has no respect for these things —only for the mind—how do you handle the child?*

You have to handle the father as well as the child. My daddy was a little like this daddy. He used to say, "If you're athletic, you're a bum. It's not productive, you'll get hurt, and you won't learn anything." Well, my daddy was wrong, and so is this daddy. Play is important whether it's listening to rock music or engaging in athletics. Naturally, there has to be a time for everything, and that includes the development of the mind. I would use this boy's interests to get through to him. Let's say he likes baseball. Okay, interest him in working out the batting averages of his favorite ballplayers. Show him mathematically how a batting slump pulls down the averages. Encourage him to follow up some ballplayers this way, using statistics, to introduce him to the practical uses of mathematics. And you can remind daddy that young David Eisenhower, who developed his mind at a high-prestige college, took a summer job with the Washington Senators analyzing the team's batting averages and other statistics. You can use the child's interest in rock music similarly to get him to utilize his mind as well as his ears. From the lyrics, develop "lessons" in spelling, punctuation, and grammar. Get the youngster to explain the meaning of the lyrics—which often are symbolic—and point out how famous authors, from Thoreau to Shakespeare, have employed similar ideas in their writings. Instead of telling him how important it is to be educated, you let him learn for himself that education can be fun and can add new dimensions to his favorite interests. The motivation is already there, you see. What you have to do is stretch it beyond its present narrow limits.

*How do you make a child live up to his name? This twelve-year-old Solomon is no wise man!*

I've known kids named Moses who broke almost every commandment handed down by their namesake, Eves who were lesbians, and Caesars who resembled wilted lettuce in the salad more than their historical counterpart. Parents often name their kids after famous people they admire in hopes that the kids will emulate their idols. Most of the time, the idea backfires. I'd guess that young Solomon here is having a devil of a time trying to live up to the high intellectual standards of his wise old namesake. He just might not be blessed with the wisdom of a Solomon —but who is? You see, a child tends to identify with the strength (or weakness) of his or her name as popularized by history and legend. Likewise, parents or relatives—even friends —may unconsciously expect the child to follow in the famous namesake's footsteps. The youngster's report card might be greeted by "That's very good, but next time you'll do even better." This is bound to make the child feel he isn't good enough. He may never be good enough because he just can't do better. This can lead to serious emotional, social, and intellectual problems. It might be a good idea to ask the youngster directly how he likes his name. At twelve, he's old enough to express his true feelings. Maybe he already has by dubbing a nickname on himself. If so, that's a sure tipoff. Use the nickname he prefers, or allow him to give himself a middle name and adopt that as his official name. This is his right. Remember, when someone asks him, "Who are you?" he doesn't say, "I'm a boy." He says, "I'm Solomon." Maybe he'd rather be someone else.

*It's impossible to tell if this six-year-old is plain stupid or simply perverse! Whatever she's asked to do, she does the opposite, like drawing in black crayon instead of red. . . . Is there something wrong with her brain?*

I doubt it. I suspect that she understands what you want her to do but prefers doing things her own way. Some kids are like that. When you tell this child to draw in red crayon and she insists on using a black crayon, she is telling you something. If you force her to use red, you aren't listening and you lose communication. Try to understand that this is her way of expressing her feelings. Some kids are told, "Study harder," and because they feel criticized, they lock up their minds and just go through the motions of studying without learning anything. Other kids are told, "Don't read that junk, read Shakespeare," but since they don't like Shakespeare, they stop reading altogether. What parents sometimes overlook—and I can't blame them because they want the best for their kids—is that when the child is doing something that isn't harmful, but is different from what the parents desire, it is best to let the child do things her way. You're worried that she will always be obstinate, will never listen, and will never learn. Stop worrying. If you force her to go your way, she's going to freeze up. Let her draw in black if she likes; and interest yourself in the drawing, not in the color. There is a dynamic learning process going on and the child needs quiet support now, not correcting. She'll begin using other colors after she gets this need to stick to black out of her system. Let this need develop dynamically and I think you'll find that she's neither stupid nor perverse.

*What can parents do to get their child to study? He just won't settle down to his job!*

Well, maybe he doesn't consider studying his job. I'm sure you've tried everything from badgering him to pleading with him. But there are a lot of kids who just can't sit down and put their minds to their studies. I've known some who copied notes from one book to another, never understanding what they were writing, simply wasting time. These are kids who can't discipline themselves to study because they are so terribly afraid that they're going to do badly anyway. Unfortunately, what happens is that the less they study, the more their parents worry and put pressure on them, but this only causes the kids to tighten up intellectually. Instead of doing better, they do worse. I suggest that you back off a bit in order to help the child find the pace at which he works best. Say to him, "Look, you're in charge here, not me. Do only as much studying as you want to do in order to do as well as you want to do. Fair enough?" That puts it squarely up to the child, you see, and this alone will give him confidence. Hopefully, it may also give him the incentive to better himself scholastically. Usually, the kid who won't study is the kid who crams the night before a test. All right, so you say to him, "Do all the cramming you want if that's the way you like to work. But I think if you began studying earlier, you'd be more confident when you took a test or got up to recite." Just plant this in his mind, that's all. Don't press the issue. The whole intent of this technique is to make the child feel that you're more interested in him for what he is than for what he does. So you don't demand accomplishment, you see. That will come when he feels ready to accomplish.

*Is there something wrong with a child who can remember dates like a genius but is otherwise quite average?*

There might be if he acts peculiarly in other ways. It is not unusual for an organically damaged or psychotic child to exhibit a remarkable memory for facts. On the other hand, this could be no more than a quirk of behavior. I've known many "lopsided" kids whose general intelligence was only average but whose minds were extraordinarily keen in one particular area. These were kids who could rattle off facts about such-and-such a date at the drop of a hat. Give one of these kids your birthdate and he'll tell you what happened on that day for the last hundred years—yet he isn't especially bright. Nobody knows the reason for this peculiarity. I call it a quirk. When it's unaccompanied by other bizarre symptoms, it often stems from a habit pattern that has been imposed upon the child. Say, for example, that a youngster was told many times, "Tell Uncle John who won the Yankee-Giant baseball game ten years ago. . . . Tell Aunt Mary what happened in American on July 4th, 1776. . . . Tell Cousin Jack the exact date we declared war on Japan." To win parental approval, the child commits to memory a whole mish-mash of dates and facts, adding to them day by day and year to year until his mind becomes a kind of depository of such information. It's something like a hobby that goes berserk. Still, it's a peculiarity that impresses people and could work to the child's advantage. So I wouldn't worry about it. I'd worry only if the child wasn't doing well at all in school and showed symptoms of brain damage or severe emotional disturbance. If he's only average, so what? Be glad he's exceptional in remembering dates.

*What do you do with a youngster who hates school, and who blames her poor grades on everyone and everything except herself . . . on her teachers, the school, the dullness of the subjects?*

First of all, be glad she goes to school even though she hates it. You're ahead right there. May schools *are* dull, and their teachers and the subjects they teach equally dull. Ideally, learning should be joyous, should be fun, but in most schools it rarely is. Despite this fact, some kids manage to do very well academically—but without ever really enjoying the subjects studied. And this can carry on right through college. I remember hearing a story about a college professor who taught astronomy. His class was graduated with very high grades in astronomy but the professor told a colleague sadly, "I know they're bright, but they'll never be great astronomers." When asked why not, he replied, "Because they do not love the stars." This kind of love comes only from the joy of learning, not from the pleasure of achieving high grades in the subject. I repeat this story in the hope that it may ease some of your anxiety about the youngster's poor grades. If I were you, I'd try to steam up her enthusiasm for one or two subjects that interest her particularly and I'd stop worrying about grades. I'd take the attitude: "When she gets to be as old as mama and daddy, nobody's going to look at her grades." It's more important that she learns to like what she's doing. But I wouldn't agree with her that the school and the teachers are no good, even if she's right. I'd say, "Well, if that's the way things are, you'll have to live with it." That puts the responsibility back on her shoulders, where it belongs. And I'd see her off to school with a smile and a good breakfast to lift her spirits and make going to school less a chore than an exciting adventure.

*How do you protect the child whose dull-wittedness makes him a laughingstock to the point where his teacher makes him wear a sign reading "Idiot"?*

I think I'd punch that teacher right in the nose! If my child is an idiot, then he's an idiot, and that's no crime. My child can't help the way he acts, but teacher can. I'd raise hell about her putting a sign on him! I feel, too, you see, and it influences my thinking. I'm sure you do the same. All right, so you have a child who's no world-beater intellectually. Well, I agree that you must protect him, but I think you have to be careful not to overprotect him. Why is he a laughingstock? Sometimes, parents become terribly sensitive to their child's shortcomings and bend over backwards to protect the youngster. Because they feel he's less than he should be, they treat him that way, guarding him, walking him around back streets, acting out their own sense of shame.

The most concerned and loving parents often act this way. As a result, the child grows up to believe that he is something to be ashamed of. But why? Nobody is really born equal. Some of us are not as well-endowed as others. It's no sin. If my child were retarded intellectually, I wouldn't be ashamed. I wouldn't try to hide the fact. I'd say to myself, "So what?" I would find other qualities in the child on which I could build my hopes. If my child behaved so foolishly that other people laughed at him, I'd say to him, "I'll go with you; let them laugh at me, too." I'd admit his difference intellectually, but I'd make it clear that he was my equal—and everybody else's—as a human being. And I think that's what you should do. It's as simple as that.

*Instead of paying attention to his teacher, this fourth-grader draws dirty doodles of male and female genitals in his notebook! Should the teacher or his parents punish him?*

He doesn't need punishing; he needs sex education, and this should come from the family if he isn't getting it at school. But even if he is, the family should support such education by dealing unashamedly at home with the subject of sex. I wouldn't regard what the youngster's doing as "dirty doodles." That may be his teacher's attitude. All he's doing is expressing curiosity about a forbidden subject. If he isn't passing his doodles around to classmates, just drawing for his own amusement, then tossing them in the wastebasket, there's no cause for concern. What I'd do is keep this interest in male and female genitals from becoming an obsession. I'd do it by showing an interest in his doodles, without admiring them and without chiding him for it. I'd use them as an opportunity to explain the biological functions of the penis and vagina. "This is what makes a boy a boy, this is what makes a girl a girl," I'd say to him. If he has a pet, I'd hold him up and say, "Here's your dog. Is it a boy or a girl dog?" As for his not paying attention in class, I wonder if that's really so. Is he productive? Does he do his work? Are his grades adequate? Many times a teacher complains, "This child never pays attention." It isn't always true. He may not be attentive enough to suit her, perhaps because she's a terrible bore, but he might be attentive enough for his own purposes. That's why I say, judge him by his work, whether he gets it done or not. If he does, leave him alone. Tom Sawyer was a daydreamer, but he was a good kid. To stop the teacher from picking on the child, tell her you're grateful to her for bringing the matter to your attention and that you're dealing with it.

# XI
## Tics and Fidgets

A youngster who twitches, can't sit still, or runs wild may be called a "nervous wreck." It's a safe bet that either mama or daddy, or both, are also nervous wrecks. The result is often bedlam arising from: 1) The child's fidgets, 2) the parents' annoyance, 3) the child's unwillingness, or inability, to obey, 4) the parents' irritation at being disobeyed, and 5) the emotional clash between child and parents that comes out of their mutual frustration. All end up as losers.

The only way to break this vicious cycle is to drain off the emotional content at the very start. A parent doesn't do this by ignoring what's happening, for this implies a reluctance to own up to the problem. A parent does this by making a decision: to overlook the fidgets, or to do something—anything from quieting the child with a bunny hug to administering a quick smack. The choice would depend on the specific situation, its effect on the child (with due consideration for the extent of any emotional disturbance or contributing organic damage), and last, but far from least, the parent's state of nerves. Excepting a show of violence, I always say that a parent should choose an alternative he or she feels more comfortable with—for without quieting down, it won't be possible to contend with the child.

Parents are likely to be more sensitive to tics and fidgets than other kinds of behavioral idiosyncracies. Why? Because nervous symptoms usually occur with greater frequency—sometimes they're constant—and parental irritation keeps building up.

Moreover, fidgets are rarely accessible to reason. You can

talk your head off, using all the logic you can muster, and not get anywhere. Chances are, though, you'll keep on talking because you hate to lay a hand on the child, maybe rightly so or maybe not. Then suddenly you run out of patience and either wallop the kid in an outburst of rage or go off on a screaming tirade that leaves you exhausted and hating yourself. And you know something? Once the youngster gets over being frightened by your outburst, he'll start fidgeting again.

So let's understand something together: a parent does become angry, has a right to get angry, and is apt to grow sufficiently angry to stop loving that persnickety child *temporarily*. So what? The best parents I know are those who can admit that there *are* times when they just can't feel love for the object of their irritation: their child. It's the *denial* of such perfectly normal feelings that make parents inadequate because it is bound to lead to their mishandling their kids most of the time. The best parents know what to do when they're steaming. They know how to demonstrate their annoyance *before* it erupts into blind rage, the real key to managing fidgety kids, as I hope this chapter will make clear. And they don't shove sedatives down the kid's throat. When they find themselves ready to go off the deep end, they take the sedatives themselves. An aspirin will do.

*It's nerve-wracking to watch a child go through elaborate rituals—turning light switches on and off, shutting doors twice, going over every capital letter he writes, counting the cracks in the sidewalk, climbing stairs over again if he misses a step—is he going crazy?*

No, but you're heading for a nervous breakdown if you go on paying so much attention to this child's rituals. This kind of behavior feeds on such attention and concern. Set your mind at ease. These rituals, which seem ridiculous, even "crazy," to you, are maddening to observe; but they fulfill an emotional need for the child. They help him drain away some very distressful feelings of anxiety and self-doubt. He may be filled with conflicting emotions and conceal his indecisiveness behind a shield of rituals, doing inane things over and over again to avoid coming to grips with his real feelings. The rituals may serve as substitutes for real desires which the youngster daren't exercise. There's the student, for example, who doesn't want to study for a test he's sure he will fail anyhow. He'd prefer to strangle the teacher if he could. But he knows he has to study. So he's in a bind. He keeps straightening his desk, piling up his books in neat rows, even measuring them with a ruler to make sure the rows of books are balanced. By balancing the books, he balances his feelings and gets rid of his anxieties. Because the rituals protect him from his hostile feelings, he can't give them up. Try to encourage him casually to omit a ritual just as a test, so that he can see for himself that nothing terrible will happen. He'll be very upset and will need a great deal of reassurance. Stay with him, keep smiling, talk about other things to distract him. When he gives up one ritual, he'll eventually give up another, and then another. Just don't press him too hard. Be gently persuasive.

*How do you handle a girl who, at any time and for no apparent reason, becomes very agitated—wide-eyed, restless, face flushed, uncoordinated—though nothing is physically wrong?*

Agitation is another way of dealing with anxiety, and its symptoms are beyond conscious control. I don't know why she's anxious, but there has to be a reason. Is she worried about school? Do her mama and daddy fight a lot? Could this youngster have done something to make her feel overwhelmed by guilt—perhaps engaged in sex play, sneaked pot, or somehow violated the family code of proper behavior? In any case, what you must do is relieve her agitation. She is under great emotional stress, from within herself or from outside herself, and needs to be comforted. Whenever she experiences one of these agitated episodes, drop whatever you're doing at the time and devote your full attention to this child. Cater to her. Stay close to her in a quiet room. Hold her if that calms her. Draw the blinds or dim the lights to remove distractions. Give her some candy or another sweet treat to chew on. In a soft voice, tell her stories about the time when she was a very little girl, for reminiscing about her early years will help make her feel like an innocent, trusting, small child again. Agitation, you see, is often an older child's way of pleading to be treated like a baby again and of shifting all notions of responsibility back on mama's shoulders. Keep soothing her until the agitation passes. Such comforting is like an act of forgiveness to her for not meeting her own expectations of herself. In a way, you're removing the stress by changing the environment she's accustomed to. She'll feel strengthened emotionally and be better able to tackle her tasks.

*What's the best way to deal with a supersensitive eight-year-old who can't stand noise of any kind and reacts by squirming, pounding his ears, and stamping his feet?*

The best way may change from day to day. One day it may be best simply to put your arms around him. On days when that won't work, it may be best to advise the family to speak softly and tiptoe around for a while. I have no idea why this child is so sensitive. I once treated a boy this age who couldn't stand loud sounds. If you clapped your hands in front of him, he'd leap two feet in the air and cry hysterically. I was able to calm him by hugging him and whispering to him. Well, this boy had become hypersensitive to noise because his fly-brained old man used him for a shooting dummy when the child was three years old. Daddy was a marksman with a rifle, and, for "sport," he shot tin cans off the boy's head to show off his skill to the neighbors. He meant the child no harm and even mama thought it was good clean fun. The boy broke down when he entered grade school. He couldn't stand any commotion, whether in the classroom, the playground, or at home. He was given sedatives, but when they wore off he was back to "normal." It took a lot of special care and attention to help him overcome his uncommon sensitivity, and he still can't endure any sustained loud sounds. Now, I'm sure your child hasn't been traumatized by such an experience as this boy's. But maybe yours is a noisy home, at least too noisy for your little guy's delicate sensitivity. Pull down the noise level and the speech level. Try to give him a carpeted room of his own to which he can withdraw to his own level of quiet. Surround him with gentleness to give him a chance to build up some immunity to noise.

*How do you stop a first-grader (who doesn't seem nervous) from vomiting at the table when there are guests?*

If he has to vomit, he'll vomit. You can't stop him. Unless there is something wrong with his digestive system, I'd guess that this child is more nervous than you suspect. I don't think he's at ease with guests. He may fool everybody because he's a good actor. But when he flips, he gives away his real feelings. That's his way of reacting. Instead of a tic, it comes out in a vomit. I knew a child who was so nervous about going to school that he threw up his breakfast each morning. Very quietly, neatly, right onto his plate. It upset me more than it did him. After a while, I learned just to hand him a napkin to wipe his chin and mouth, give him a glass of water, and bring him a clean plate. He would then eat half a slice of toast and sip a little hot chocolate. And he would go to school. That's all I did for him. I didn't make a big thing of his vomiting. After a few weeks, he stopped vomiting. Apparently, his nervousness subsided when he became accustomed to school so that it no longer seemed so threatening. I'd suggest that you try the same approach with your youngster. If it embarrasses you too much if he flips in front of your guests, then you'd better feed him separately. It won't help him to see you uptight. Have him join you at the table only when the guests are people he truly likes and feels comfortable with. You'll feel more comfortable with such guests yourself if the child should vomit during mealtime. Relax. This too shall pass.

*What's wrong with a preteenager who embarrasses his family by refusing to button his collar, tighten his belt, or even pull up his socks, complaining, "I'm being choked!"?*

He must feel squeezed to death by what he considers too

many demands made upon him. Nobody may be making such demands, but this is probably how he feels. He's probably a boy who takes himself very seriously and feels straitjacketed by responsibilities that other kids would take lightly. Look around, see if he isn't feeling "tight" in other ways: his spending habits (Is he tight with money?); his bowel habits (Is he constipated much of the time?); his attitude to tests (Does he tighten up?). I think you'll find such clues, all of which suggest that he feels crowded in by pressure to achieve, conform, or whatever. This youngster is probably too demanding of himself. You'll get him to loosen up if everyone around him loosens up by permitting him wider latitude behaviorwise. He reminds me of a high school track star I knew whose coach was very critical. The young fellow was a good sprinter but always lost the big race, disappointing himself, his coach, and his family. He got to the point where he felt so tight that midway around the course, his legs crumpled under him and he'd yell, "Owwww, my legs are coming off!" He couldn't take the pressure. He needed reassurance. He couldn't get it from his coach, so his parents gave it to him and he became a better runner. He told me, "I'm trying my best and my folks are real proud of me." I think your boy needs reassurance, too, and as little criticism as possible. If he isn't embarrassed by his "tightness," you needn't be. Ease up on him and on yourself.

*If a child crows like a rooster when playing games, is he nervous or worse?*

It's probably an outlet for strong feelings, but instead of expressing how he truly feels, the child disguises his feelings by crowing. He might want to retaliate against a playmate, for example. However, he might be afraid to hit him so he crows instead to let steam off, at the same time letting the other kid know he's a pain in the neck. Somebody gripes him, he gripes him back. Annoyance for annoyance, you see. The crowing becomes a kind of "crapping" game. You bug him so he "craps" on you by crowing. If he didn't crow, he'd boil over, or twitch, or do something worse. So if crowing is all he does, I wouldn't make too much of it. Above all, I wouldn't make fun of him by crowing back even though I might feel like doing it. I've known kids who crowed in the classroom to get attention, to express boredom, and just to get on teacher's nerves. That's a different problem because the crowing takes place in a work situation, not a play situation. Many perfectly adjusted kids—and adults—crow like a proud cock-o'-the-walk when they beat a tough competitor in a game. It's a spontaneous thing. However, since this child seems to crow more deliberately and it obviously has you upset, you might try to rechannel this kind of vocal response to another kind. Give him a toy motorboat when he's in the tub and push it over the water, going "Putt-putt-putt." Make him a paper airplane, toss it up in the air, going "Wheeeeee!" Since he has a need to express his feelings vocally, you see, give him new ways to do so. Sing aloud at home. For no reason at all, burst into song. Now and then, have the whole family sing along with the radio or phonograph. Eventually, with this kind of conditioning, the child may learn to sing instead of crowing.

*Everybody talks about this six-year-old who's forever fidgety, picks at his eyelashes, cracks his knuckles, bobs his head, all sorts of annoying tics. . . . What can be done?*

Nothing very quickly. He can't stop fidgeting. You have to bear it or try to minimize it. What you do depends on how much these fidgets bother you or others. If they get you so uptight that you've begun to take your feelings out on the rest of the family, you'll be better off taking some positive corrective steps. This doesn't mean swatting the kid's hands or bopping him on the head. It also doesn't mean calling his attention to what he's doing every time he does it and yelling, "Stop that!" The less attention you pay—or *seem* to pay—the better. Here's a reconditioning technique I've used in similar cases with success. The basic idea is to shock the child at the moment he fidgets so that he'll associate that shock with that particular tic. Let's say his eyelash-picking bothers you most. All right, the moment you spot him doing this, bang your fist hard on the table —without looking at the child. In other words, don't you associate the fist-banging with the tic; let the child come to that conclusion himself. Use this technique every time he picks his eyelashes. It will stop him short and, eventually, discourage his eyelash-picking. This is an adaptation of behavioral conditioning therapy that uses small electric shocks in place of fist-pounding. Now I won't promise that the child won't replace one tic with another. But at least you might eliminate the one you find most nerve-wracking. Use other "shock treatments"—anything from slamming a door to loudly clearing your throat—to deal with other tics. But don't expect to remove all his fidgets. These are his defenses, his means of coping with life situations. Remove some of his anxiety by making the home more fun and everyone in it a bit more tolerant.

*How do you help a little girl get to sleep who begins to itch every time bedtime rolls around?*

Try giving her a cool bath before she turns in. Be sure her pajamas are soft so they won't irritate her, and loose so they won't bind her. These procedures will take care of her physical needs, and if she feels more comfortable physically, that could help her feel more comfortably emotionally. She might simply be "itching" to stay up a little longer. Some kids nag mama or daddy for glass after glass of water just to stay up. Others keep saying goodnight over and over again, or keep going to the bathroom, or suddenly find things to do, like feeding the dog. All are subterfuges to stay up a little longer. Well, you allow a child such liberties once, twice, and then you say firmly, "Now it's time for bed." You may find that the youngster will feel more secure with a small light burning in her bedroom. Leave it on. Lots of kids fall asleep faster with a light on than with it off. Some like to read themselves to sleep. If, despite everything, her itching persists, sit with her a while, read to her, talk to her, but limit the time you spend with her. Say, "Okay, honey, I'll stay with you ten minutes and then I expect you to feel tired enough to roll over and go to sleep." Have other members of the family take turns at this task so that she doesn't become used to you alone. The whole aim is to calm her down to make her itching subside. Never tie her hands even if she scratches herself until she bleeds. Soothe her skin with a cold damp cloth, and hold her hands in yours affectionately. One or several of these techniques should help her relax and stop feeling itchy. And if she gets less sleep than you feel she should have, don't worry about it. She'll make up for any lost sleep when she gets tired enough. In fact, if postponing bedtime will eliminate the itching, I'd postpone it.

*It's weird to see a nine-year-old walk around with a light bulb "to see better"—though it isn't connected to anything! Is this merely playacting?*

It might be. Does he laugh about it, or take it seriously? Is it an occasional thing, or something he does consistently? Do you think he does it to get a rise out of others, or only to amuse himself? If you answered "Yes" to the first parts of these questions, the child's behavior might be nothing more than playacting. But if you answered "Yes" to the second parts of these questions, I'd be concerned that it might be symptomatic of something serious, perhaps a developing psychosis. Try to nip this in the bud, not by telling him to stop, but by tricking him out of it. Buy an electric cord with a socket on one end into which you can screw a bulb. Plug the other end into the electric outlet. Give this to the child to walk around with, and let him switch the light on. That's a real light, not a delusion, but you don't tell him that. You help him discover it for himself. Let him play with *this* bulb in the evening with the room dark so that he can enjoy the fun of making the bulb light up. This is not the same as pointing to a lamp, switching it on and making the bulb light up. He might not associate the lamp with the bulb with which he walks around. You have to let him use the connected bulb in the same way that he uses the unconnected bulb to establish a meaningful association. If you simply let him continue walking around with a dark bulb, deluding himself that it's lit, pretty soon he's going to believe it, if he's having difficulty coming to grips with reality. If the technique I've suggested doesn't cause him to break his weird habit, then you have to give up trying to handle this by yourself. You'll have to bring the boy to the attention of a psychiatrist.

*We're all nervous wrecks because this little girl is a nervous wreck! She rocks by herself a lot or else sucks her thumb. Is there some remedy?*

Yes, all of you stop being nervous wrecks. This little girl isn't rocking or sucking her thumb to bug you, so don't take it personally. It's not your fault, she's not mad at you, and there's nothing for you to feel guilty about. Of course it bothers you, but if you can accept the fact that her rocking and thumb-sucking have nothing to do with you, it will bother you less. I'm not suggesting that you simply put up with it. There are things you can and should do, but you have to understand what's going on. All right, consider the thumb-sucking. Every once in a while, say offhandedly, "Take your thumb out of your mouth, honey." Don't say it frequently and don't say it angrily. At other times, try to get her to change direction. You do this by ignoring—or *seeming* to ignore—it and switching her to another activity. Say to her: "Will you get me that book on the table?" "Come and help me prepare lunch," "Go see what time it is," anything to make her change direction. As for the rocking, what I would do is bring it out into the open, not by making a fuss over it, but by rocking with her. I'd participate by suggesting, "Let's rock together for a while in my rocking chair." Every day I'd set aside certain times for rocking and call it "rocking time." I'd announce such times: "You can rock now, this is rocking time." I'd turn it into a specific activity, you see, to help the child establish some control over her need to rock by controlling the times for that activity. There'd be times to rock just as there are times to eat, watch television, or indulge in other activities.

# XII
# Being Fear-Ridden

Some fears are reasonable; others aren't. It's reasonable to be fearful of standing on the edge of a cliff; it's unreasonable to be afraid to go up to the top floor of the Empire State Building. It's reasonable to exercise caution when crossing a busy intersection; it's unreasonable to have to hold somebody's hand to do so. It's reasonable to feel edgy walking alone on a dark street at night in a high-crime area; it's unreasonable simply to be afraid of the dark. Too little fear in certain situations can be careless and foolhardy; too much can lead to paralysis. The child, for example, who is appropriately tense when taking a test will think twice before answering; but once he is immersed in the activity, his tension will disappear, leaving him in command of the situation.

When still in infancy, all reality seems terrifying to a baby; and the tot must be soothed and coddled until he learns to trust those giants hovering over him who are his parents. Little by little, he tests the real world around him—the darkness, the strange sounds, the shape of things—and learns that they do not threaten him. As he develops, learning to walk, talk, and manipulate his environment, he achieves a sense of mastery over his environment, and the fears subside.

However, some children for one reason or another never manage to rise above their fears which may not become clearly evident until school age. Such kids may be terribly shy, even antisocial, fearful of the impressions they are making on other people and clinging to their mamas' apron-strings. Or a sudden terrifying incident might traumatize a child, implanting deep fear where none existed before. The recent California earthquakes had this effect on thousands of children who began experiencing nightmares, fantasizing that the walls would come tumbling down, and becoming so boxed-in by dread and depression in some cases that they talked about suicide.

Now, you can't reason a child out of his fears. It won't work. Psychoanalysis tries to trace such fears back to their basic origins in order to drive them out. This takes a long time, lots of money, and doesn't always succeed with children. What parents can do is to place themselves between the child and whatever is feared. This can be done simply by saying, "Don't worry, honey, I won't let the building fall on you, I won't let the flame hurt you, I won't let the doggie bite you." In addition to such reassurance, fearful kids must be encouraged to express their fears aloud, talk about them, in order to relieve their feelings.

Any child who is victimized by unreasonable fear is a problem not only to himself but also to his parents. I'm not going to try to track down the source of such fears in this chapter, but I am going to spell out some ways of making them manageable to the point where both the child and you are in control.

### *What makes a boy too cowardly to fight back?*

Some kids won't fight back because they've been told too often to keep their hands to themselves. They're afraid of what they might do to the other kid if they ever let go. Others don't fight back because someone in the family has been pushing them to be heroes and they aren't so sure they measure up. Don't be too quick to call your child a coward. And for God's sake, don't ever use the word "coward" to belittle him. It will only make him feel worthless and may even turn him into a bully. The child who won't stand up to other kids when he ought to is a child who is paralyzed by fear. It won't help to buy him a punching bag. But it might help to encourage him to take a few jabs at his father. It could build up his self-confidence and help him get rid of some of his fear. If his daddy accepts his aggressiveness, and the punches that go with it, the boy may stop being afraid to fight back. A father who's a good actor can work the child into a corner, forcing him to fight his way out—and allowing him to do so. Even more important, though, this kind of child should be encouraged to fight in other ways than with his fists: for his rights at home and at school. If he learns to fight for his rights in one way, he'll be able to fight for them physically as well should the need ever arise. Let him argue to make his point when you disagree and let him stand up to his teachers with whom he has just disagreement. This will build up his ego and make him feel more manly. It will each him the value of self-defense.

*If a small child is fearful of policemen, is he likely to grow up to hate them?*

It's possible. Most of us hate whatever frightens us. If I were you, I'd try to help this child get over his fear of cops as quickly as possible. I know how upsetting this can be because I had such fears myself as a child. I grew up hearing my friends say, "If you're a bad boy, the policeman will arrest you." Even my daddy used to tell me jokingly, "You better be a good boy, Monty, or I'll call the cops!" It was no joke to me. The fear became so strong that years later, when I took my driving test, I flunked it four times because the man who gave it to me was a state trooper. His uniform paralyzed me. I was a damned good driver but couldn't do anything right—went through red lights, forgot my turn signals, and kept jamming on my brakes because I hadn't anticipated the "Stop" signs. Now, I don't know where your child's fear of cops came from, but I'm pretty sure the uniform is scaring him. Is he also afraid of the mailman, doormen, bellhops, soldiers, and sailors? Could be. Nevertheless, deal only with his fear of policemen. You can't say, "I won't let the cop hurt you," because that implies that cops *do* hurt kids. But you can reassure him that the cop is his friend, there to protect him from trouble and to help him cross the street safely. Single out a friendly neighborhood officer and tell him of your child's fear. Arrange to pass his beat when your child is with you and, holding tightly, protectingly, to your child's hand, stop to chat with the officer. By prearrangement, the policeman should then squat down and chat amiably with the child. Repeat this several times with this one policeman, not with the whole force, until your child feels comfortable with cops. I did this by myself. With your help, your child will do it faster, and his fear of cops will be erased.

*Shouldn't a child be forced to get along with relatives even if she dislikes them? It's terribly embarrassing to see her shrink back from members of the family!*

I know how you must feel. But think how the child must feel. I learned long ago to trust children's feelings. When they dislike an aunt, uncle, cousin, or even a grandparent, enough to shrink away, that relative must have done something, wittingly or unwittingly, to make such kids fearful. So you can't say to the child, "But Uncle George loves you," because the youngster can sense whether Uncle George really loves—even likes—her enough to put up with her. The best of kin have personal problems that make them crotchety some of the time, but you can't expect a small child to understand and make amends for this. A youngster's feelings are too primitive. It is the more mature and sophisticated relative who should understand the child rather than vice versa. When relatives truly like a child, they'll go out of their way to demonstrate their affection. Some go too far, in fact, and become so overenthusiastic that their aggressiveness frightens the child. The point I want to make is that you're entitled to feel embarrassed, but your embarrassment will disappear if you think less about the effect of your child's attitude on your relatives and more about the child's feelings. Consider, too, the possibility that the youngster may be very sensitive to the kind of relationship you have with these relatives. Sometimes conversation at home suggests that a relative hasn't been too considerate of one or both parents, and a child will shrink back from this relative because her loyalty is to mama and daddy. I say, nuts to the relatives! Side with the child to give her strength.

*Is it normal for grade-school youngsters to be fearful of growing up? Both brother and sister are terrified of the future!*

It may not have been normal in your childhood and mine, but these are different times. There *are* lots of goings-on that inspire fear: the H-Bomb, constant war, crime in the streets, deterioration of the environment, and so on. Television, radio, newspapers, magazines, movies, even popular song lyrics, tell us Doomsday is just around the corner. Kids know what's going on. They even feel the pinch of inflation in their homes. And the fears start building up at a very tender age. In a New York City public school, ordinary kids were asked what they wished for most. Here are some typical answers: "I wish that right now the entire earth was destroyed and this miserable thing ends because we'll all be wiped out by a bomb anyway"; "I wish that the moon would become a melting pot so we could all fly away and get away from here"; "I wish I could wake up. This world is only a dream. In the real one, there are no poor or bad people." Do you sense the fear behind those answers? Get brother and sister involved in working for more than just grades to give them a sense of excitement, of doing, so that they'll abandon the hopelessness that's making them fearful. Switch them from the usual extracurricular activities to volunteer work helping the underprivileged. Read them stories from the newspaper about young people who are doing great things in medicine, politics, and social work. Don't try to hide ugliness, but do try to spotlight the good things going on to put down ugliness. If you give these kids some purpose in life, they'll stop being afraid to grow up because they'll have something exciting they can look forward to.

*How do you help a child who's so fearful of people that he's constructed a dream world and chases imaginary butterflies?*

You must try to get him to convert his escapist fantasies into something real and positive. When he chases imaginary butterflies, for example, you don't say, "Cut that out, you're crazy!" It would be cruel and only frighten him more. You drag him back to reality by manipulating him so that he'll start chasing real butterflies. This won't be easy. It will take time. First, get him interested in real butterflies by showing him pictures in a book. Take him to the museum and show him some mounted butterflies. He'll go along because he's interested in butterflies. Then buy him a net and a kit for collecting specimens. Show him how to use the equipment. Go with him to your garden or the park or some nearby field and help him capture real butterflies. When he traps one in his net, he'll feel a sense of great accomplishment. So will you, because the child has made contact with reality. After he's collected a specimen or two, sit with him and help him mount them. Point out the different species as he builds a collection and encourage him to show them off to other people. Select the kinds of kids and adults who will react with warmth and enthusiasm. Both parents should show keen interest in the child's achievements. It will take months of dedicated effort before the youngster transfers his interest completely from imaginary to real butterflies. When that happens, you've got him back in reality. By that time, he'll have sufficient faith in you and his admirers to give up his fear of people.

*Believe it or not, this seven-year-old still believes in ghosts! Should he be allowed to sleep with his head under the pillow?*

Well, the ghosts don't seem to be keeping him awake nights. As long as he sleeps, what difference does it make how? Just be sure he can't suffocate himself with his pillow. He might not be as afraid of ghosts as you suspect or else he'd be up half the night looking for them. Sometimes, you have to take what a kid says with a grain of salt. "I'm scared of ghosts," he says, maybe because he thinks he should be (he might have read about it in a storybook), or because he knows this gets you all concerned and he likes to see you worry over him. Now, if his belief in ghosts was causing him to sleep badly, or not at all, then you'd have to prove to him that there are no ghosts. At bedtime, you might leave a small light on while you go thrashing about the room searching for ghosts. "I've looked everywhere," you tell him, "and I can't find any ghosts around." If he wants to keep the light on for reassurance, let him do so. Or if he wants to leave his door open a crack, let him do that, too. In the morning, come into his room and say, "You know, I stayed up half the night looking for ghosts, even came in here and looked, and didn't find any at all. I guess if there are any ghosts, they don't want to have anything to do with us." You see, you don't tell him there are no such things as ghosts, because he won't believe you. You just tell him there aren't any in his room, or your room, or anywhere else in the house. That will take the edge off any fear he has and, eventually, shake his belief in ghosts altogether. Give him every chance to prove he's still right. Let him join you in a ghost-hunt at bedtime. When his curiosity is satisfied, he'll agree to turning off the light, closing the door, and sleeping with his head *on* the pillow.

*Name it, and this child is afraid of it—bridges, trains, tunnels, elevators, high buildings. . . . What can be done?*

Take them one at a time. It's a tall order, but every fear you help the child to overcome minimizes the others. Start with the fear that offers you the most opportunities to work with. If, for example, you live in an apartment house, the fear of elevators must be a burden not only to the child but also to you. At the same time, the elevator is always convenient for use when you need it to help the child cope on a step-by-step basis with his fear. Here are the steps to follow: 1) Tell the child you're going to help him stop being afraid of elevators, 2) have him time how long it takes you to go up several flights non-stop in the elevator; then have him time how long it takes him to do it running up the stairs; you'll win, 3) walk in and out of the elevator with him; let him push the buttons that open and close the door; do this many times without going up or down, 4) when the whole family is together, ask him to go up just one flight with you, then walk the rest while you ride, 5) take him shopping, load him down with bundles, and, when you arrive home, ask if he'd like to try the elevator, but don't force him to if he refuses, and 6) invite him to bring some friends in; they'll want to take the elevator and he'll probably be ashamed not to join them. All these steps are to familiarize him with the elevator. Familiarity drives out fear. When he's conquered his fear of elevators, walk with him around the highest building you can find until he feels at ease beside the towering structure. Then take him into the lobby to watch the crowds of people going in and out of the elevators. I think you'll find he'll want to try an elevator ride if you go along to give him confidence. Work similarly with his other fears. With each success, the others will be easier to lick or will vanish by themselves.

*How can a youngster overcome a fear of germs that makes her afraid to kiss or even shake hands?*

She needs a lot of help from her parents. In homes where I've seen kids who had a phobia of germs, I found that there had been a great deal of emphasis on cleanliness and health. Now, its important for a youngster to be clean and to stay well, but when the family is preoccupied with such things a sensitive child may feel terribly threatened by the prospect of anything less than perfect health. Dirt and germs are to be avoided at all costs, you see. This situation can develop from circumstances beyond the parents' control—a major illness in the home, for example, that puts the whole family on edge and plants panic in the mind of a little girl. Whatever the reason may be for the youngster's fear of germs, I think it would be a good idea to go about deliberately creating a new atmosphere in the home. Deemphasize cleanliness. Let daddy say aloud one night, "I'm too tired to take a bath this evening," and let mama reply, "Then don't take it. You can skip a night." Put a ban on all cautionary remarks like "Be careful," "Don't dirty the furniture," and "Bundle up." If any member of the family gets a cold or has a minor accident, make very little of it. Don't rush in with an armful of aspirins, antiseptics, and bandages. Be patient. It will take a while before the effects of this deemphasis on cleanliness and health are felt by the child. You can also be specific. If she turns away, for example, when you try to kiss her goodnight, say with a smile, "Honey, I kissed you all those years when you were a little baby and you never once got sick. And I remember how you hurt your finger once and I kissed it to make it well. But the kissing didn't make it better, and it didn't make it worse either. It only made you feel better. That's all that kissing does." Make a point like that once in a while.

*If a boy of twelve is a real worry-wart, worried especially about dying and starving (he stuffs himself at every meal!), is there some way to put an end to these worries?*

Yes, but it's not going to be easy. By twelve, these worries have had time to establish a hold on him and become part of his basic outlook on life. A worry-wart is fearful of life in general and this includes everything from a fear of failure to a fear of not being loved. Dying then becomes a way to escape such fears. At his age, his emotions are reachable through his intellect. Reason with him by making a study of life-expectancy tables that show him statistically and scientifically that he has a long way to go before he dies. But be honest with him. Say to him, "Son, everybody's a little afraid of dying because it's an adventure into the unknown. But you don't see mama and daddy worried about dying. When it happens, it happens, that's all. The important thing is to get the most you can out of life." This rational approach should eventually penetrate his understanding if you also help him to enjoy life more. Take some of the stress out of his day-to-day existence. If he's a grind at school, tell him to ease up. If he saves every penny, encourage him to spend some money on himself. Surprise him with a treat now and then: a movie, a dinner out, a Sunday picnic, a gift (that has absolutely no educational value). In other words, try to bring more fun into his life. If he wants to stuff himself, let him. But say, "There's plenty more whenever you want it; you don't have to eat it all at once." And try to enjoy life more yourself, and to show it. There's a contagion in enjoyment that rubs off on the kids naturally. When kids know that mama and daddy are having a good time at life, they'll have a good time too.

*How do you cure a little girl of being superstitious?*

"Cure" is the wrong word. Superstition isn't a sickness; it's just an irrational way of looking at things. I mention this because I don't think it's a good idea to confuse superstition with mental illness, even unconsciously. Your goal should be simply to have her give up believing in myths. But if there's anything we hate to give up, it's a belief in myths. I've known people who've knocked on wood, then told me quite seriously, "I'm not superstitious, but why take a chance?" Or they rationalize: "I'm not afraid to walk under ladders, but I just don't like to." Well, they aren't fooling anybody but themselves. They pretend not to be, make jokes about it, and tell their kids that superstitions are ridiculous, but they continue to believe . . . and their beliefs rub off on their kids. They aren't even aware it's happening until they begin wondering: "Why is that kid so superstitious?" If I were you, I'd give the child opportunities to test out her superstitions. But first I'd set her an example. If my daughter won't walk under a ladder, all right, then I'll walk under a ladder while she watches me. "See," I'll say, "nothing happened. That ladder's perfectly harmless." Of course, I'd make damned sure that there was nothing on that ladder that could fall down on me when I walked under it! Then I'd say to my little girl, "Come on, walk with me, try it for yourself." Then after she did that, I'd give her a kiss and say, "See, all you got out of it was a kiss!" I'd make her laugh. This would poke fun at the superstition—with her approval—and take the fear out of it. When it comes to superstitions, reasoning won't help; you have to use a sense of humor.

# XIII
## Sex Games with Adults

I don't think you'll find a boy or girl anywhere who, sometime during their childhood, didn't fantasize about making out with mama or daddy, their adult friends, or other members of the family. Sigmund Freud believed it, and I believe it, too. I know I did, my chums did, and most of the kids I've known admitted that they did. Of course, thinking about doing something and actually doing it are two very different things. My concern in this chapter is with kids who may try to do something or do try, and with parents who are worried that they're going to try.

For the most part, grown-ups like to forget that they ever entertained such fantasies because they're considered taboo. Here I'd like to reiterate that what's taboo is not the fantasy, but the acting-out of the fantasy. However, parents worry about their kids growing up normal, and if they suspect the fantasy, they're likely to make too much of things that don't need worrying about. At the same time, parents are often unaware of how their own behavior might be seductive to their child and, instead, go to extremes to correct the child who doesn't need any correcting at all.

On the other hand, there are times when parents do have something to worry about but fail to recognize what's going on. I've seen clear signs of trouble in families where one or both parents were either too shy, too permissive, or too preoccupied to intervene in unhealthy erotic situations involving their kids and themselves or other adults. I believe in giving a child the benefit of any doubt but there is always the danger of bending over backward so far that you don't see what's happening in front of you.

It isn't always a simple matter to separate the harmful from the harmless. It's especially difficult for parents who themselves are too extreme, too proper, or too indulgent. If you're going to be perfectly honest with yourself—and you ought to be to spare yourself a lot of future headaches—ask yourself whether your own attitude to sex has made you an extremist. It's a good rule of thumb to assume that very proper parents are apt to jump the gun at the slightest embarrassment by a child who's feeling his oats sexually, while very indulgent parents are apt to dismiss any but the most blatant kinds of sexual acting-out.

We're dealing with an aspect of behavior that parents can't readily discuss with anyone. Even family doctors who are taken into a parent's confidence are likely to feel so embarrassed that they just pussyfoot around the situation, or else blow an incident up all out of proportion and label the child a pervert. Few bother to suggest consultation with a psychiatrist who feels comfortable discussing offbeat sexual behavior. So, deprived of professional guidance, most parents become too ashamed to search out competent advice themselves. They try to believe that their fears are inconsequential and that the problem will disappear. Well, maybe it will, and maybe it won't. It's more sensible for parents to understand what's happening and do something about it themselves. Here are some insights into sex games between kids and adults, and some techniques for dealing with them.

*Is there something wrong with a youngster who gets an erection in the bathtub while having his back scrubbed by his grandmother? She was terribly shocked by his immodesty!*

Modesty won't stop him from having an erection. If he's old enough and he feels stimulated, he's going to have one. Since he didn't bother to conceal it, he's probably still quite innocent about sex and may not even know what to do with an erection. He doesn't even seem curious enough to try to find out. Another child might wave his penis around proudly to show it off to grandma and say in wonder, "Golly, I'm growing!" It's also possible that the youngster might be aware that he is having an erection but may have a very wholesome attitude to natural biological functions. He may not demonstrate a sense of shame because he doesn't feel ashamed, he feels comfortable with grandma, she's one of the family. The problem here is grandma. Any boy old enough to have an erection is several years too old to have his grandmother give him a bath. Kids should have privacy in the bathroom, whether they're in the tub or on the pot. If they want company, they have their fantasies. If they want to have erections or masturbate, it's nobody's business except their own. You can't hold junior responsible for being stimulated by grandma's touch. A kind of covert mutual seduction takes place that is unhealthy for the boy. It can become especially unhealthy if grandma should become so shocked that she screams at her grandson for having an erection, slaps him for it, or acts disgusted. I'm sure grandma means well but keep her out of the bathroom when junior's in the tub.

*Should you allow your eight-year-old's cousin, a homosexual of college age, to hug and kiss the child hello and goodbye when he sees him?*

If it's nothing more than a kind of father-and-son bear hug and nip on the cheek, I wouldn't make an issue of it. But if the kiss is on the lips, is prolonged, or if the hug is accompanied by stroking, there are elements of homosexual seduction in such displays and they should be discouraged at once. Is the cousin obviously feminine in speech and manner? If so, he'll know that you are fully aware of his homosexuality, and it is your right— and parental responsibility—to tell him to avoid such demonstrations of affection. Do this kindly, with tolerance for the young man's differences, but make it clear that just as you respect his uniqueness you expect him to show respect for your own sexual standards. If the cousin's homosexuality is not apparent, or is merely suspected, just manage to be around when he greets your son and see to it that such greetings are very casual and perfunctory. It isn't wise to leave a child in the company of a known or suspected homosexual. One or both parents should always be present to "mask" any seductive gestures. By this I mean that the parents should immediately distract the child's attention, when, for example, he is engaged in a rough-and-tumble game with the cousin where there is opportunity for fondling. Homosexuals, even with the highest motives, may by their unconscious attitudes influence a small child whose innocence makes him vulnerable to the unexpressed, but implicit, feelings of older people whom he likes and would emulate. Through the technique of masking, you intervene between the child and the homosexual in a variety of ways that conceal or inhibit actions that could distort the child's sexual self-image.

*Is it proper for a mother to walk around in bra and panties in view of her eleven-year-old son or to let him zip up her blouse?*

It could be in your house if you've been casual about nudity all along. Still, being half-dressed is not the same as being undressed. It is usually more provocative, unless it's commonplace for mama and daddy to go around in their underwear. As for zipping up mama's blouse, this could have decidedly sexual overtones just as does the situation of a father who likes to lounge in bed on Sunday mornings and have his young daughter crawl in to scratch his back. Nobody but daddy should zip up mama's blouse, and nobody but mama should scratch daddy's back. It isn't healthy for the kids to assume these roles. Something else happens here that doesn't directly concern the kids, but it can affect the parents' attitudes to each other, and this in turn will affect the kids. I'm referring to the possibility of jealousy between father and son, or between mother and daughter. In underprivileged homes where entire families are forced to live in one or two rooms, the economic circumstances dictate a more casual relationship between the sexes, parents and children.

Even so, there are times when such closeness serves to override social taboos and permits incestual desires to be acted out. Middle-class cultural standards generally cause families to be rather uptight about nudity in the home. Efforts to be more casual prompt some middle-class parents to conceal part of their nudity with their underclothes. This is like telling a child, "There's nothing to be ashamed of in going around without clothes provided you wear some clothes." It's double-talk. It doesn't cause a child to feel more comfortable about being naked; it only makes him eager to see more nakedness. The fact that you raise the question suggests that you don't feel comfortable either.

*If you find your six-year-old being fondled by her uncle, who is three times her age, what can you do besides throw the pervert out of your home?*

Your first impulse should be to protect the child, not to punish the boy. This is a damned difficult choice for a mother to make, I know, when she comes upon the kind of scene described. But you have to separate the two quickly, not by bawling out the fool of an uncle, but by distracting your child's attention. You might call to her and tell her to get you something from another part of the house, just to get her out of the room. Then tell the uncle that you disapprove of his behavior and for him to leave at once. Cover his exit by telling your daughter that he had to go home. What you do next depends on how intensive was his fondling and how affected she was by it. Did he play with her vagina? Did he rub against her and, if so, did he have an ejaculation? Did he entice her to touch his penis? Think about such questions but don't put them to the child. Wait for her to volunteer information. If she doesn't, she probably wasn't deeply affected. If she does, make your answers brief, simple, and casual. If she giggles and tells you that uncle touched her "peepee," or whatever she calls her vagina, don't smile because that will imply approval or at least tolerance for the fellow's behavior.

Just keep a straight face and say, "That was foolish of him. You know how to make peepee by yourself." A six-year-old will accept that. Don't permit yourself to become overconcerned. Play it cool and there is little chance that the child will suffer any permanent effects from the experience. I would mention the incident to the boy's parents, not for punitive measures, but to make them aware of their son's character weakness so they can take steps to help him.

*Isn't it harmful for a parent to be too demonstrative to a child of the same sex?*

How demonstrative is too demonstrative? If you mean cuddling a small child, I say no, it's not harmful, in fact it's very healthy. If you mean titillating the child with tickling, for example, then I say yes, that could be harmful. I think you're too worried about demonstrating affection. All kids need the warmth that comes from being held, hugged, and kissed. You don't convince a child of your love just by telling him, you see. You have to show it, by your general attitude, and by your touch. Too much reserve will make you seem cold, distant, even rejecting. Both parents should feel comfortable about demonstrating affection. A boy needs reassurance of his daddy's love, and a girl of her mama's love. Naturally, as kids grow up, displays of affection taper off. A teenage boy prefers a handshake to a peck on the cheek. A teenage girl busses her daddy, he doesn't buss her. Affection should be spontaneous, not ritualized. Kids shouldn't be compelled to kiss mama or daddy every time they go out, come in, or go to bed. A schoolboy wins a ball game and both parents give him a congratulatory smack on the cheek; a girl has her first date and both parents give her a kiss for good luck. Such shows of affection are fun and let children know that they're genuinely loved. Homosexuality doesn't arise from a parent's good-natured hug or kiss. It's more likely to result from a parent's fear of expressing affection so that in later life the children, starved for affection, will seek out mother-substitutes or father-substitutes to get it.

*How do parents face a child after he's caught them in a sexual act by walking into their bedroom?*

With a little embarrassment, that's all. This happens more often than you might imagine. Sex is something that should be very private but parents are human and do get careless. Look at it this way—you were "caught" but you weren't doing anything wrong. What you do depends on how old the child is, but in any case you stop the act short. If the child is very young, no more than six or seven, he's not as apt to be as suspicious as you think. If you get the feeling that he doesn't have the slightest inkling of what's been going on, say to him, "Hey, you want to talk to mama and daddy? Come on over and talk to us if you like." You'll be frustrated, and I'm sure damned annoyed, but you can make up for lost time later. Right now, welcome the child and spend some time with him. On the other hand, if the youngster is older and wiser, he will suspect something. So you can't afford to lie to him. Be outspoken to the point of saying, "This is private. We'll see you later." Send him out of the room, there's nothing wrong with that. He knows what's going on. Afterward, you come out and join him. Don't bring up the subject. Wait for him to do so. If he does, say, "Well, making love is part of being married." Don't make a big deal of it, but be honest with him. If he doesn't bring it up, drop the subject. But if it happens again, then you'll know that the child's curiosity has not been satisfied, and this is why he's interfering with your privacy. He should know better. He doesn't, though, because sex is still a mystery to him. It's time to educate him. Talk about sex as a commonplace biological phenomenon, an important part of living and loving. And teach him good manners by setting an example—always knock on *his* door before entering *his* room.

*Should you correct a boy whom you've caught looking up your friend's dress while she was sitting on the sofa?*

Not if she's been spreading her legs inviting him to look. In that case, she needs correcting, not the child. Some women—even a mama's best friends—are sometimes seductive. They can stimulate a child or daddy himself. I wouldn't think twice about telling such a woman, "Pull down your skirt and zip up your blouse." She has no right to tease your child that way. Remember, kids are human, too, especially growing boys who are beginning to experience their sexuality. On the other hand, if this child was on his hands and knees, using some pretext for his curiosity, it's sneaky and he needs correcting. But don't make an issue of it while your guest is there. Just distract him by saying something like, "Will you go down to the candy store and get the afternoon paper." When your guest has gone, take him aside and tell him frankly that you saw him looking up your girl friend's skirt. If he's old enough to look, he's old enough to be talked to this way. But don't say to him, "You mustn't do that." Instead, say, "We don't do that." There's a difference. In the first remark, you put all the onus on the boy. In the second remark, you allow him to share the onus with everybody else, including yourself. This puts him on notice that sneakiness is out of bounds with the family and goes against their way of thinking. This gives the child support and makes it easier for him to align himself with the moral code that you choose to establish for him. You can utilize this same technique, using "we" instead of "you," to induce him to change other behavior that could be unhealthy.

*A girl's daddy admits to getting an erection when carrying his daughter on his shoulders piggyback, but says it's only natural, he's not doing anything wrong. Should he nevertheless stop the game?*

Yes, he should find other games to play. A father can get a hard-on with his daughter, but he shouldn't go on playing the kinds of games that give it to him. Sooner or later, she has to get the message, and that will distort her maturing processes. The same thing goes for a mother who feels stimulated by her young son's caresses. She may not be doing anything, but whatever is happening should be brought to a stop. It's unhealthy for the kids; and even if the parents mean well, it's going to be unhealthy for them, too, in the long run. I'm sure this girl's daddy means no harm. Still, he ought to stop this game. The taboos of civilized society serve to keep parents and children at a decent distance from one another automatically. Where the kids are adopted or are stepchildren, the distance might be shortened because social taboos don't operate in the same way. But even with one's own kids, there has to be a respectable distance maintained in order for parent and child to respect one another's privacy. Sometimes a daddy goes to sleep. His daughter crawls into bed beside him and rubs against him, and he gets an erection, not knowing who it was that caused it. When he opens his eyes, and sees his little girl beside him, he automatically loses his erection because of the built-in social conditioning that makes such behavior taboo. If he doesn't, he's out of bounds with normal society. In this respect, such behavior is unnatural because it doesn't conform to the rules. Well, if daddy won't conform, why should daughter conform when she gets older? In the problem posed here, daddy means no harm; but in being stimulated, he's stimulating daughter. The game should stop.

*What should a mother do when she senses her little boy is snuggling her breasts and is giving indications that he wants to play doctor?*

You have to sidestep the situation without being obvious. Here's a boy who has the hots for his mama. Well, it wouldn't do to embarrass him, but he has to be restrained. You don't do this forcibly or by chastising him. You just turn aside, that's all, and beat him to the punch. When he reaches out for you, grab his hand and say, "Hey, let's take a walk." Turn him off not by showing disapproval but by switching him off to something else. You have to discourage this kind of contact. Moreover, if the child is mature enough to feel these desires, he's old enough to take notice of the way you dress. It might be a good idea for you to dress as unprovocatively as possible. Consider it a step you have to take to play down any possible stimulating effect you might be having on the youngster. But don't reject the child. By making a play for mama, he's making a plea for physical contact. I wouldn't get too uptight if I were you. I'd give him a hug, but not an impassioned one, giving him the warmth and affection that he seems to need so badly but retreating before he can become stimulated. I've known kids who've tried to touch their mama's and their daddy's private parts only because their sexual curiosity had been stifled. Don't be ashamed to introduce your son to sex. Show him pictures of the sex organs and tell him what reproduction, and love, are all about. With his curiosity satisfied, he'll only need the warmth that comes from elementary contact and nothing more.

*Is there anything to worry about when a girl behaves flirtatiously with older men such as her uncles and her daddy's friends?*

Yes, this is something to worry about. A girl who's old enough to flirt is old enough to get into trouble. Parents have a tendency to write off such behavior as merely playful but I've learned from experience that this kind of playfulness can lead to trouble. My suggestion is that an uncle, or one of daddy's most trusted friends, say to her kindly, "Now, look, I'm very fond of you and want very much to be your friend. But that's all. Do you understand?" The girl who flirts will understand. It's better to have this come from another person, but if this can't be managed, it should come from you. Say to her, "Honey, you're embarrassing Uncle Joe (or Cousin Bob, or whomever), and I want you to stop it." This is no time to play games. You have to make yourself clear. This is a situation where parents have to take a firm stand and attack the problem directly. If this girl —ten, twelve, fourteen, or whatever her age—is allowed to continue being flirtatious, she'll eventually beguile some older man. This isn't healthy. If I were her daddy, I'd tell her, "You're behaving foolishly and I won't stand for it. If you keep it up, I'm going to be very angry and punish you." I would take it upon myself to supply the controls that she seemed to lack. This kind of attention—even though it threatens punitive measures—may give her enough strength to stop being flirtatious. When a parent gets this strong, you see, some of the strength rubs off on the youngster responsible for such a show of strength in the first place.

# XIV
## Drawing into a Shell

Loners and wallflowers are embarrassing to parents who, understandably, want their kids to be outgoing, friendly, and popular. In a world that's become smaller and more crowded, it would seem that opportunities to socialize would be abundant. Ironically, however, people—and that includes kids—are becoming more alienated from one another through the intervention of computers, tape recorders, and vending machines. It's become easier than ever to get lost in the crowd, and there's no loneliness more devastating than the kind that comes from having people crowding about you without you. Kids can feel lonely even in their own families.

However, all kids are not outgoing at all times, and some aren't outgoing at any time. Neither attitude means they're abnormal. A great many children prefer to be by themselves and indulge their creative talents. They're doing something reasonable, you see, and that's perfectly healthy. They may lead lonely lives by your standards, but not by theirs. Many writers, artists, musicians, scholars, and scientists spent withdrawn childhoods but used their aloneness productively.

The real problems are those kids who are too withdrawn, too shy, too "blah" for their own, or for their parents', comfort. Often, they're disagreeable. Most times, they're just sad without apparent reason. Some sulk in a corner, others retreat into a world of make-believe, and still others simply won't communicate. These are generally kids who, for one reason or another, don't trust people. You need a lot of perseverance to deal with them.

The unfortunate thing is that such youngsters don't use their self-imposed privacy to their advantage. Perhaps this is what hurts a parent most of all. Unless they're reached, and as early as possible, these are the kids who will grow up to be daydreamers, social isolates, and exiles from life.

This chapter is about such children. Both sexes. All ages. Kids who don't communicate because they don't want to, or because they can't. Kids who draw into a shell and live in a world of their own. Kids who may be on the verge of becoming psychotic. They leave you, the parent, all tied up in knots. You want to bring them out into the fresh air and you can't. You want to make them smile and you can't. You want to make them understand how much you love them and you can't. Well, I hope to show you how you can.

*When a child's only pleasure is to go off by himself, search the sky for airplanes, and stare at them intently until they disappear from sight, could he be losing his mind?*

He could, but I doubt that he is. It might be dangerous, however, to let him continue this interest to the exclusion of other activities. He's withdrawing too far. I suspect that for some reason he has lost his faith in human beings. When he gazes at airplanes this way, he's expressing a longing to go off into the wild blue yonder where no other human can touch him. I'll bet he's hard to talk to, that he doesn't look you in the eye when you speak to him. I've known many such kids, so distrustful of people that they slither away from everybody and wind up in a closet or up a tree. I remember one little boy who used to build tunnels in the dirt that he could disappear into. These kids feel safer alone, you see, because of their dread of people. You have to persuade this child to come out of his shell, and give him opportunities to test his relationships and gradually learn that they aren't threatening to his well-being. Do this by initiating a one-sided relationship, with you doing all the giving

Overlook any mistakes he makes, any chores he fails to carry out, any show of stubbornness. Don't lecture. Use silence, along with a smile, in place of conversation when it is appropriate, when the child wants to do the talking. You must get across the message that you are content to accept him exactly as he wants to be. Your whole purpose must be to kindle a relationship of mutual trust. Don't stop him from looking at airplanes; look with him. Then try to involve his interest in a game that will amuse him and subtly teach the pleasure that comes from cooperation. Let him win. It may teach him to be selfish. Fine. He'll thrive better selfish than withdrawn.

*If you keep badgering your ten-year-old to make friends and she snaps back, "You have no friends, why should I!" what can you say to her?*

Whenever you don't know what to say, just shrug. Your little girl's remark is like that of the kid who crows to his daddy, "I saw your old report cards and you didn't do so hot; why expect better from me?!" When kids talk this way, they put you on the defensive. I never write off such comments because they teach me a lot about myself that I wasn't aware of by pinpointing my weaknesses. Here, I have a feeling that you may not have as many friends as you would like, and your child senses this. Isn't it possible that this is why you've been badgering her to be more popular? Most parents do want their kids to have more of everything than they have, be it money or friends. If the shoe fits, wear it, and be proud. It reflects the concern of a good parent. What you should say to her is, "I have all the friends I want. Do you?" This puts her on the defensive. She may sass you back or storm away from you. Let her. You've made your point. At some less emotional moment, you can mention that this or that girl might like to be friends with her and that you think she'd find such friendships fun. Let her know that you'd welcome the girls if your daughter would like to have them visit; but don't press the issue. And don't expect her to become a social butterfly. A child who questions you as she has will never covet popularity. Some kids prefer to be choosy and restrict themselves to one or two good friends with whom they feel comfortable. Your daughter sounds like such a child and should be encouraged only to this degree.

*How can you make an uncommunicative child talk to you? The silence is maddening!*

You can't "make" him talk to you. Communication doesn't come by insisting on it. Does this child speak to anyone else? If not, you can assume that he feels too unhappy to make conversation. If he talks to others but not to you, then you can guess that he is angry with you for some reason. Try to discover what's bugging him. A third party—the father, a brother or sister—may have to intercede to break the silence. Once he opens up, allow him to express his anger. Don't aim for a civil conversation. He has to get whatever is bothering him off his chest. Stand there and take it while he pours out his feelings. It will hurt, but you can take it better than he can. Keep remembering that if you didn't mean so much to him, the child wouldn't bother to turn against you in the first place. After he's cooled down, you'll be able to talk together like human beings. Now, if this child has stopped talking to everybody, not just to you, let him sulk for a few days to give him time to work through his feelings. If he remains mum and sullen, go to him and confront him alone in his room. Quietly, uncritically, tell him exactly how you feel, how his silence is upsetting you. Present him with one argument at a time, first your concern, then your frustration, and finally your displeasure. If he still won't talk, to you or to anyone else, the time has come to make him mad enough to express his feelings, to rage, to curse, even to strike back. Surprise him with a sudden hard whack on the backside that will shock him into reacting. He'll probably go off on a tirade. Let him. When he's spent, give him a hug to let him know how glad you are that he's decided to talk again.

*Is there some way to brighten up a sour-puss who's down in the dumps a lot, hides in her room, and won't say how she feels?*

I wouldn't ask directly, "How do you feel?" I'd try to pin her down to specifics: "Are you sad about something?" "Are you worried?" "Are you mad at anybody?" This way she could answer "Yes" or "No," just with a nod or shake of her head. At the same time, I'd learn what in particular is bothering her and be able to deal more understandingly with her feelings. But I'd try to reach her this way outside of home, maybe just taking a walk together, or on a short drive to the edge of town, or over at the neighborhood soda fountain. What's needed here is a change of environment, a change of pace, a bit of novelty or excitement to help loosen her tongue. It's a "con" job, you see. So you don't just come right out and ask her questions. You surround her with activities that are upbeat and fun, and with pleasant chitchat. The idea is to perk her up just enough to let you sneak your way into having a heart-to-heart talk with you. Often, a sensitive child becomes disappointed in herself because she hasn't done well at school, or because she has misbehaved and maybe has been punished too severely, or because something has happened in the family that upsets her. A change of scene, a fresh approach, and a good "con" job can work wonders on a sour-puss.

*Should you turn away from a child who keeps insisting, "Leave me alone!" and to whatever you say, replies, "I don't care!"?*

Yes and no. Let me explain. Your child is in a kind of deep-freeze. He wants you to get off his back, yet if you turn away he'll feel rejected. He's in a bind, you see, and is putting you in a bind. All right, then, you have to give him just enough rope to feel independent but not disowned. Let him withdraw to the safety of his room, his bed, wherever he chooses. Don't pry. Just wait, standing by, out of sight and out of earshot but alert and ready to step in when the child needs you. He will know you're standing by him even though you're out of his way, you see, and that's what he wants. Like other kids in a bind, he speaks in a code of his own. When he tells you, "I don't care," don't you believe him. This is a cover-up for his true feelings. He really cares too much about something. You have to be perceptive and observant, waiting for the right moment to make a move toward the child. The right moment is when he stops objecting so strenuously to your presence. You have to play this touch-and-go, feeling your way. Very often, when a child like this has had enough, he will suddenly begin to sob because he's feeling very sorry for himself. It's not unhealthy for him to cry. The tears release some of his pent-up feelings, and are a sure sign that he is coming out of his shell. When he's able to cry, he's getting better, not worse. Some parents misinterpret such tears, feeling guilty and resentful, and shout, "What are you crying about now!" Believe me, when he cries, be glad. The child wants you.

*How do you bring out a pretty girl who's too shy to go to parties or, if she does go, stands on the sidelines to the chagrin and disappointment of her parents?*

Well, you could be very direct about it and say, "Go to the party, honey, you'll have a good time." She might go to please you as she seems to have done in the past. But apparently she hasn't been having the good time you thought she would. This hurts a parent, especially when daughter is pretty. It seems like all that prettiness is wasted because the girl is too shy to socialize. But if she isn't comfortable at parties, her good looks will be hidden behind a sad, unsmiling face. I think it's a mistake to encourage her directly to attend parties. It's better to go about it in a roundabout way or maybe not do anything at all. If she's shy, that doesn't mean she's a social isolate. Does she have friends? Does she belong to any clubs at school? Does she attend small gatherings of two or three school chums at one or another's house? If she's able to do any of these things and enjoy doing them, she's not a loner and I wouldn't be concerned about her shyness. She'll bloom in her own good time. On the other hand, if she's a frightened little fawn who pulls away from people, then you have to help bring her out. Entertain more at home and invite your guests to bring along their kids. Don't force your child into friendships but try to create situations that make friendship and friendliness inviting. If there's another little girl in the neighborhood of similar age and disposition, you might be able to effect a friendship between the two. Remember, too, that if your daughter makes constructive use of the time that she's alone, she may be very happy being by herself. That should make you happy, too. She'll find her way, maybe not to the top of the popularity pole, but high enough to suit her needs and personality.

*What can be done when a child refuses to eat with her family, making her brothers and sisters angry?*

You just say to her, "I'm going to serve dinner, honey, and we'd all like you to eat with us." If she refuses, then you say, "Well, I wish you'd think about it some more. You can skip dinner if you like but you might be awfully hungry. I'm not going to serve you separately, honey. The next meal will be breakfast." This is going to be very hard for a mama to do. You aren't going to like to see your child go hungry. Well, try to bear it. Remember that it doesn't hurt to miss one, two, or even three meals. You have to get the child to understand that you eat together as a family. You see, the problem is complicated because of how this youngster's brothers and sisters feel. They're angry because they think to themselves: "Why can she get away with doing whatever she wants? She isn't entitled to any special treatment!" It's natural for them to be jealous if their sister seems to be on mama's preferred list and eat whenever she likes. Now I don't know *why* she doesn't want to eat with the family. Is she restless at the table so that the other kids pick on her? Is she overpowered by the personalities of her brothers and sisters so that she feels left out of things? Is she a fussy eater and subjected to continual pleading to eat this and eat that? Any such circumstances could make her reluctant to eat with the family. Try changing her position at the table. Seat her beside someone who will pay her attention but not criticize her. In order to coax her to the table, have a special little treat for her—and very firmly instruct the other kids to welcome her enthusiastically. Tell them, "If you want your sister to eat with you, be nice to her or I'll feed her separately whether you like it or not." You have to deal with *all* the kids to help the one.

*How can you get a withdrawn child to tear himself away from the TV set?*

Since he can't control his viewing habits, you have to control them for him. Don't be afraid to turn off the TV set even if you have to put up with some temporary flak from the child. But don't just leave him on his own then or he'll only withdraw into his shell all the more. Help him find a happy substitute—not homework—that will give him pleasure as well as keep him occupied. Don't hesitate to reward him for changing his behavior patterns. For example, you might turn off the set, announcing, "It's time to mow the lawn. I've got a shiny quarter waiting for you if you do a good job." You might be able to get him interested in building model airplanes, pasting recipes in a book for you, or some other busy activity, preferably the kind that will become a project to which he can devote a chunk of time each day. Feed that interest by making a game out of rewards. Give him a button for every half hour he spends on his project. Let him save his buttons and trade them in for special treats—two buttons for a candy bar, ten buttons for a record for his phonograph, twenty buttons for a Sunday trip to the zoo and all the hot dogs and popcorn he can eat. Set up your own reward schedule to wean him away from the TV set with as few withdrawal symptoms as possible. At the same time, regulate the hours permitted for television. You may have to cut down your own viewing time to set an example. If the set is in the living room and too much of a temptation to the whole family, consider moving it into your bedroom. Sometimes a set is too conveniently situated and it becomes too easy to twist a knob at any time of day or night to "see what's on TV." Let the child have his stretch of TV each day, but no more, while he learns to participate in what life offers instead of being merely a spectator.

*Is something wrong with a first-grader who sulks around wishing he could fly, and breathe without air, and crazy things like that?*

No. He has a pretty wild imagination, but that's not unusual for a child his age. I know some grown-ups who wish they were Superman and could fly. It's a perfectly harmless fantasy that gives them a little breather in the rat race of making a living. When a child wishes he was Superman, he's telling you that he's still a little bit wary of reality and that he'd like to master it more successfully. I wouldn't be concerned if he held his breath or wished he could fly. But I would be worried if he actually tried to fly by jumping off a tree or table. In that case, he'd be demonstrating an inability to distinguish what's real from what's imaginary, and that is dangerous. I'd also be concerned if the child lived in his imagination too much of the time. He could have imaginary friends, even talk to them if he likes, just so long as he remains aware that it's only make-believe. I get the impression that this youngster is merely playacting, engaging in wishful thinking, and more or less testing his mastery of the environment. The only thing that troubles me is the sulking. This could signify a drive away from reality. I'd counter this possibility if I were you by playing realistic games with him that would stimulate his intellect, rather than his imagination—number games like Bingo or Lotto, for example. I'd also encourage him to express his feelings on paper, by drawing pictures or writing poems and stories. This would put some skin and bones on the products of his imagination and make them substantial, tangible, real. In other words, harness that imagination to bring out his creativity where he can see, touch, and feel results, even if he has no more talent than it takes to build a house with blocks.

*Should a sixth-grader be allowed to shame his parents by withdrawing from participation in traditional activities like saying grace, saluting the flag, and dressing up to go out?*

If you feel ashamed, you can't allow it. Just don't make the mistake of thinking that the youngster is breaking with tradition to shame you. This is not the same world that existed when you and I were kids. Our parents merely had to protect us from the elements, teach us moral values that were generally accepted everywhere, and give us some direction in life. It's a whole different ballgame today. Changes in all aspects of society have come so quickly that the stability of the family has been severely undermined, as have the values and traditions that mama and daddy grew up to believe in. It's hard to raise young kids today because they're beginning to question those values and traditions. At the same time, they haven't found new ones to replace them with and are searching for substitutes they can believe in. Their frustration comes out as protest and rebellion, and their mamas and daddies don't know whether to be permissive or authoritarian. Well, there's a time to be both. If you can understand that this protest is not directed at you personally but is just a symptom of the child's own confusion, his behavior won't upset you so much. You'll know what steps to take and feel confident in your decisions. The key is to maintain sufficient discipline to keep the child—and the family—from flying apart. If he won't say grace, he should show respect for those who do by bowing his head silently. If he won't salute the flag, he should simply stand at attention. If he won't dress up, he should dress neatly and wear clean clothes. With this technique, you preserve your parental authority while the child preserves his sense of independence.

# Postscript to Parents

I never intended this book as a manual on how to bring up children. That would be presumptuous of me. It would amount to my telling you to raise your kids to please me. But I don't have to live with them. You do, and they have to live with you. This book is intended as a kind of survival manual for parents, something to turn to when situations are getting out of hand. I've tried to offer some techniques to help you cope with situations too vexing or too embarrassing to admit to anyone except yourself. It's based on my belief that kids, through no fault of their own, can ruin parents just as parents, through no fault of their own, can ruin kids. Crises occur because they are often invisible in their developing stages. I hope that my book has given you some insights you can use to spot crises in the making, and some means to abort such crises before the whole family reaches the breaking point.

Remember that no one knows for sure what it is that makes one child more "impossible" than another. You can have six kids —five will be a cinch to raise and one will give you fits. Well, if you've ever planted a garden, you know that all flowers don't bloom alike. It's the same with children. I have a feeling that difficult kids are just more sensitive and so become more vulnerable to what happens around them as they grow up. They could be more sensitive because of some organic damage or physical handicap, and not all physical deficiencies are obvious—hypoglycemia (low blood sugar) or hyperthyroidism, for example. So the first thing you must do is give your difficult child a complete physical checkup and have corrected any organic problems that exist.

If there are no organic problems, or if the child remains hard to handle despite medical attention to any physical deficiencies, you have to find ways to contend with the youngster's unpleasant behavior. Now, you can have him tested and retested psychologically until Doomsday. This won't help the child or the other kids in the family, although it may appease some of your anxieties. Your task still is to cope, whatever the reasons may be for the child's difficulty in adjusting to the ground rules of the family, with or without professional guidance.

But just as there are constitutional differences between children, so too are there constitutional limitations on parents. Just as one child can "take it" better than another in the same family, or can do better in school, or whatever, so too can one parent frequently "take it" better than the other, and so too can one mama brush off annoying behavior more easily than another. The more difficult the child, the more you have to sway with the hurricane. This can put a big strain on you, and not everyone can stand up to the same amount of strain. Now, I know you aren't an indifferent parent or you wouldn't be reading this book in the first place. And if you aren't indifferent, you must be motivated to take on your problems and resolve them. And if you're motivated, that's all the credentials you need to do the job. All right, then, if you haven't been as successful as you'd like, I have a feeling that it's simply because you've misjudged your goals or your capabilities.

## HOW FAR IS TOO FAR?

You have to be realistic. Kids can't be made over, nor can you. Some parents set themselves impossible goals and, at great cost to themselves, try to do the impossible. Instead of achieving their goals, such parents become anxious and resentful, and succeed only in making a bad situation worse. Any success they do achieve may be obtained at such high cost to themselves that in time these accomplishments backfire on both themselves and their kids.

Do you think you might be trying to do too much? Does your child have physical or mental limitations that prevent adjustment or improvement beyond a reasonable point? Are you unconsciously comparing this youngster with one who is better endowed physically or mentally? Do you think you might be trying to "re-do" this child without sufficient regard for his basic personality?

Be honest with yourself. If your answers to any of the above questions is an unqualified "Yes," then you are setting your child—and yourself—an impossible task. Reduce your expectations. Reassess your goals to match the limits of your child's capabilities. Over a period of time, you may be able to do more, but you can't rush the process. Go slow.

Besides respecting your child's limitations, you have to respect your own. If you don't, you're bound to feel that you're being used by the child, and then nothing you try is going to work. Why? Because you're resentful, your efforts aren't appreciated, and you feel guilty for feeling as you do. Well, when you feel guilty, your self-esteem will drop so low that you won't be able to do anything right. This is why you have to know your limitations. It might help to ask yourself these questions:

1. Can I relate to this child without getting too uptight to make rational decisions?

2. Am I able to control my impatience if my child doesn't respond immediately the way I want him to?

3. Can I feel comfortable going along with a technique agreed upon by my spouse and me?

4. Do I have a thick enough skin to shrug off my child's unreasonable attitudes?

5. Can I forgive and forget without harboring grudges that will affect my attitude—not my feelings, just my attitude—as a parent?

6. Am I willing to live by the example I choose to set for my child's behavior?

7. Can I put up with dirty looks and worse from friends and neighbors without penalizing my child for "offending" them?

8. Have I begun to feel a bit less irritable and a bit more understanding?

9. Am I really ready to try new techniques, not just to help my child, but also for my own peace of mind?

10. Do I truly believe I'm a better parent than my child's behavior seems to credit me for?

Don't expect to reply with a resounding "Yes" to all these questions. If you can say "Yes" to half of them, you're already in command and should be successful. Why? Because you have a pretty good idea of your weaknesses and your strong points. It will help you to cultivate those qualities you need to deal more easily with a difficult child.

## USE YOUR ASSETS

Once you abandon unrealistic expectations—of yourself and of your child—you'll automatically raise your tolerance level, take your time in trying to bring about permanent change, and grow a thick enough skin to absorb the punishment, criticism, and ingratitude that often are the price of parenthood.

Your greatest asset is your sense of humor. With it, you can overcome a sense of shock, bewilderment, or upset, because a sense of humor acts as a shield that prevents sticky situations from getting to your gut. Your sense of humor is also your child's greatest asset. If there can't be laughter, let there be a smile, a grin, a chuckle. All set up a healthy contagion in the home that tends to take the edge off wayward behavior.

It also helps to think of yourself as a creator. You mothered or fathered this child. That's a considerable accomplishment that should give you a sense of power. Such a sense of power can move you to do great things. Sometimes, it helps to "psych" yourself by thinking of your child as "normal but different." This gives you a fresh perspective to work from and an excuse to reshape your attitudes. With that kind of perspective, you'll begin to appreciate your own importance in your child's life.

It's also a good idea to keep alive your sense of wonder. By this I mean that you have to keep reminding yourself that you are a human being, with all the strengths and weaknesses that go with being human. It's becoming too easy to avoid the responsibilities of being human by allowing ourselves to be seduced by the second-class wonders of our scientific age—the tape recorders, television sets, computers, and vending machines that annihilate or sterilize communication. You have to keep reaching out to people so that you'll keep *feeling,* even if it's only misery, because from misery you can still move up to joy, but from being frozen you can't move anywhere. Don't get bogged down by going the second-class route via machines even though it's sometimes a more painless way of living. In time you'll lose your sense of wonder and that will seal you off from your child, who (thank God) still thrives on wondering at things.

**DISCIPLINE**

To change a child's behavior, you must reeducate the child. To reeducate the child, you must teach him the value of self-discipline. To get this idea across, you must deal out discipline yourself. It could take the form of a word, a disapproving look, the deprivation of a privilege, or a whack on his bottom. You have to let him know that you're displeased with his behavior and you believe that he can do better. This disciplining has to be done on the spot, at the time the child acts up. Don't say, "I'm going to tell your father when he comes home." If you as the mother would prefer that the child's father handle the situation and he's around at the time, let him do so. But if he isn't around, don't put things off. Handle it yourself. Right then and there.

If you feel more comfortable structuring your discipline, then balance your scoldings, criticism, and punishments with smiles, praise, and other shows of affection—and be sure that the latter outweigh the former. You just can't go on belting a child even if he keeps setting fires in the living room. He'll just get used to the beltings and become convinced that that's all he's good for. You have to balance your reactions by complimenting him on his good points. It's the only way he's going to believe he's good for something, not just a good-for-nothing. This is the thing you have to get across to such a child, that he is good for something, if not all of the time, at least some of the time.

### COMMUNICATION

Exercising proper discipline is one way of communicating with a child. There are other ways as well. I don't mean simply making conversation. You can talk to a mixed-up kid for hours without communicating. When I talk about communication, I'm talking about a two-way street. You give, and you get in return. Somewhere in the process, mutual understanding takes place.

I suggest that you be more liberal in rewarding the child than in punishing him. By this, I don't mean bribery. I mean rewards for actions that demonstrate a child's efforts to adjust to the rules of the family, not because you bribed him but because you encouraged him to change his behavior. He's entitled to be rewarded for such efforts. By responding in an approving way, you communicate your *feelings* to the child. This is the essence of communication.

### YOU NEED A SAFETY VALVE

There are times when the pressure builds up, especially when you and your spouse don't see eye to eye on how to deal with the situation, or if you're strictly on your own because you're divorced or widowed. At such times, you aren't going to be able to cope unless you can let off steam. Be sure you do. If you don't, you'll take out your feelings on your child; and this will only aggravate the situation.

Remember the old "wailing wall"? That was the first treatment center for overburdened mamas. Well, I think you need a "wailing wall" of your own. Reserve a private corner in your home for yourself. When you feel things crowding in on you, go over to that corner and pour out your frustration. You'll feel better after a good cry. I'm old-fashioned enough to believe there's more therapy in a good cry than in a whole bottle of aspirin. Whatever it is that's bothering you doesn't get pushed down; it comes out.

I remember one time I resorted to a very childish tactic of kicking at a door to get rid of my frustration. I banged up my big toe in the process, but I felt a hell of a lot better emotionally. I realize that this is one of the things you want to stop your kids from doing, but there are times when such ridiculously childish behavior can save a parent's sanity.

You have to have a safety valve to keep from falling apart or from becoming overinvolved with your child's feelings. Preserve your own peace of mind by letting kids have their feelings. Don't try to take them into your psyche. If you don't keep a healthy emotional distance between yourself and your child, you will only share his misery. That's not your task. Your task is to stand above it so that you can influence him to change. The formula to strive for is equal parts of empathy, sympathy, and emotional distance. That's the ideal way to handle feeling. It requires a lot of concentration and conscious effort on your part.

Still, it is better to feel more than to feel less. If you didn't feel, you would be a machine and could be programmed to do anything. Fine. But in order to get results, your kids would also have to be machines so that they could be programmed to receive what you dish out. Well, you can't do such-and-such to get such-and-such results because you *and* your kids *feel*. Communication and reeducation begin when you tune in on each other's feelings. But without a safety valve, there's a good chance that you'll blow. You need such occasional respite to recoup your own feelings, or all your resourcefulness and ingenuity won't be worth a damn.

## IF YOU'VE REACHED THE END OF YOUR ROPE...

So you try to work miracles and they never happen. You try this and that and nothing seems to work. You get to the point where you can no longer be an optimist without feeling like a fool. You decide you have to be a superparent, and you can't. Despite your most heroic efforts to help your child, you can get nowhere. You've had it.

If you've reached this point, it might be sensible for you to seek professional counsel, not for your child, but for yourself. Psychotherapy might help to put you in a more coping frame of mind. I suggest this also because it is generally easier to find help for yourself than to search out competent help for your child. With a bit of support, you could very well refresh your attitudes and take on your child's problems more effectively. Then, too, many parents feel more embarrassed to seek help for their kids than for themselves. So, if this is the most comfortable road for you to travel, take it.

Unless your child is utterly unable to cope with school, I'd suggest that you see to it that he remains in regular classes as long as possible. But if he can't cope, then raise all the hell you can to convince the school authorities to transfer him to a special education class with a less demanding curriculum and, most important, a concerned and understanding teacher. Such a teacher, in fact, can perform minor miracles even in an ordinary class, and if you can effect such a transfer without the need for a special education setting, by all means try this first.

Now, in many classrooms, drugs are being given kids who are hyperactive. And there are doctors who will run the gamut —from telling you that a seriously disturbed child will "outgrow" his behavior problems, to putting him on drugs to make such problems invisible—and I don't go along with any of this. Drugs will make a child less of a bother but they bypass the real problem and just might turn the unfortunate child into an addict. I don't believe in drugging a child into submission. The purpose of any drug should be only to lower the child's threshold of resistance just enough—and just long enough—to enable one to get through to the child's feelings.

There are children—severely brain-damaged, physically handicapped, or clearly psychotic—whom even the most devoted parents cannot cope with and for whom it is best not to be "tolerated" at home. Such youngsters belong in residential treatment centers. I admit that these are hard to find, good ones are even harder to find, and harder still to find are ones that parents can afford without putting themselves into economic strait jackets. In any case, the decision to send a child to such a residential treatment center should not be made too quickly or too lightly. You know your child—and yourself—and you should make the final decision. I am sure that you will have to wait a long time —perhaps many months, even a year or more—before your child can be admitted. There just aren't enough facilities, good or bad, to meet the demand. Until such round-the-clock assistance becomes available, I suggest that you use this book to work out stopgap techniques while you wait.

If you feel there is no alternative except professional treatment—for yourself or your child, or both—seek the attention of a competent psychotherapist. Such competence is generally measured by an M.D., or Ph.D. (in psychology), after the therapist's name *and* membership in the American Psychiatric Association, the American Psychoanalytic Association, the American Academy of Psychoanalysis, or the American Psychological Association. Still, this is no guarantee of success. In my view, psychotherapy is as much an art as it is a science. One professional, or one therapy technique, might be effective with one child but not with another. A great deal depends on the communication between therapist and child.

Ask your family doctor to recommend a professional person with whom he is acquainted personally. Or ask a friend. If you are unable to obtain such recommendation, contact the nearest large hospital (preferably one connected with a university) or mental health center, and ask to see one of their psychiatrists. If this isn't possible, get a referral to a clinic or private doctor from your local mental health association; or call your nearest family service agency and ask them for counseling. These are non-profit organizations in business to help you. If all counseling services are too busy to see you, tell them you can't wait and to suggest an alternative. Hustle them to do so if you have to.

Don't sign a lifetime contract with anyone. If you do see a psychotherapist—or if you bring your child to one—and don't feel that you're getting results after a dozen sessions, you could be wasting your time with that therapist.

You'll have to go the same long route to find a residential treatment center for your child if you feel the youngster would be better off away from home. If you feel this way, don't let yourself become guilty about sending your child "away." It is more considerate of you to know when you've reached the end of your rope than to deny it to yourself and everybody else.

However, before taking such drastic measures, it might be a good idea for you to take another look at the questions in this book that apply to your child's problems. Work your way through the index to pinpoint other material that could be helpful. Give yourself and your child every possible chance. If it is at all possible to manage things on your own, by all means do so—not because you're better equipped than the professionals, but because a good professional person is hard to find. But if you truly feel that you've given all you can, and nothing is working, then don't delay in searching for professional counsel. Whether you help your child directly, on your own, or indirectly through somebody else, you can chalk it up as a personal triumph for yourself.

Believe me when I tell you that your child will be the first to let you know this. From your child—and from no one else—will you get the satisfaction that comes not simply from being proud of your child but from having your child proud of you.

# Index

Acne, 61-62
Aggressiveness, child's, 39, 44, 48, 141, 152
Alienation, 163
Allergy, 62
Aloneness, 163
Anger, child's, 39, 46-47, 105
Anus, 52
Anxieties
  appeasement of, 176
  child's way of getting rid of, 21
  draining away feelings of, 130
  easing child's, 46
Athletics, for boys in development stage, 101-02
Attractiveness, 100
Authority, parents', 37, 114

Babbling (incoherently), 119-20
Balance, upsetting emotional, of child, 17
Baths, calming influence of, 102
Behavioral idiosyncrasies, children's
  bed-wetting, 26-27
  bizarre erotic, 29
  blasphemous, 25
  chewing discarded chewing gum, 22
  compulsive, 106-07
  crawling on the floor, 27
  customary, pattern, 39
  disrespect for other people's property, 110
  drooling, 23
  embarrassing, 27
  erotic, 29
  eyelash-picking, 135-36
  fear-ridden, 139-49
  feet-stamping, 132
  fidgeting, 135, 136
  fingernail-biting, 21
  fist-banging, 136
  fits, 41
  fly, opening and closing, 24
  gutter words, 22-3, 50
  hair pulling, 21
  influence on, 16, 34
  licking, 21-22
  lip-picking, 21
  lying, 69-80
  messy habits, 23
  nose-picking, 19-28
  "oddball" sex, 94
  pants-wetting, 26
  provocative habits in, 20
  psychotic, 54
  rambunctious, 47-48
  reckless, 81-92
  seductive action, 37
  slobbering, 23
  smelling, 21-22
  sneaky, 78-79
  techniques to alter, 7, 23-24, 25, 27, 28
Berserk, 43, 44
Bingo, 172
Birth control pills, 35
Blindness, 59, 65
"Boyishness," girl's, 98
Busts
  comparing of, 31
  development of, 32

Calmness, of parents, 39
Cheating, 69-80
  humiliation of parents by, 72

# INDEX

Chewing gum to stop nail biting, 21
Child(ren)
  accident-prone, 87
  annoying habits of, 19, 20
  and his teacher, 182
  angry, 43
  antisocial, 139
  at odd with society, 10
  attitudes toward, 6
  babbling incoherently, 119-20
  bad habits of, 19
  bad manners, 72
  biting his daddy, 41
  biting his nails, 21
  brain-damaged, 118
  breaking bad habits of, 19
  bullying, 112-13
  called "sissy," 86
  calming the, 39
  careless, 82
  cheating, 69-80
  communication between parent and, 19, 166, 180
  considering the personality of the, 35
  constitutional endowment of, 39
  cowardly, 140
  "crazy" rituals of, 130
  crippled, 65
  defective, 59
  deformed, 60
  destroying parents' self-esteem, 40
  destructive, 105-15
  disfigured, 63
  disrespect of, 40
  doing foolhardy things, 89-91
  dull-witted, 125
  dumb, 65
  emotionally disturbed, 15
  eyelash-picking, 135-36
  fear-ridden, 139
  fidgety, 130, 135
  fist-banging, 136
  frustrated, 39
  going berserk, 43, 44
  handicapped, 11, 59, 60, 65
  hangups, 18
  hating parents, 45
  hating school, 124
  hemophiliac, 68
  "hopeless," 11
  hunchbacked, 66
  hyperactive, 47, 182
  "impossible," 7, 16, 175
  intellectualy tightened up, 123
  intolerance of, 40
  jealous, 42
  "lopsided," 124
  lying, 69-80
  messing, 50
  misbehavior of, 41
  mischievous, 114
  mishandling of, 130
  mongoloid, 64
  motivated to change, 10
  "normal," 15
  nervous, 21
  organically damaged, 123
  out of parental control, 105
  patsy, 85
  personality of, regard for the, 177
  physical defects of, 15
  playing with matches and knives, 86
  provocative habits in, 20
  psychotic, 54, 123
  questioning values and traditions, 172
  rambunctious, 47-48
  reckless, 81
  reeducation of, 7, 40, 118, 179
  regard for personality of the, 177
  residential care for, 15
  respecting the limitations of the, 177
  retarded, 15, 118
  restraining of, 7
  ripping off his clothes, 196
  running away from home, 83
  self-discipline, 17
  self-mutilation, 21
  sensitive, 169
  sexual "oddball," 93
  shoplifter, 77-78
  shy, 139, 163
  smoking pot, 84
  stealing, 49, 69-80
  superstitious, 148
  tantrum(s) of, 39, 40, 42
  tattling, 75-76
  taught value of acceptable behavior 43

## INDEX

Child(ren) *(Continued)*
  treatment, 15
  troubled, 11
  uncommunicative, 166
  understanding of, 15
  unpredictability of, 40
  "upbeat," 48
  upsetting emotional balance of, 17
  using gutter words, 22-23, 50
  victimized by unreasonable fear, 140
  withdrawn, 163-64
  with emotional problems, 118
  with lesbian tendencies, 97-8
Cleanliness, deemphasized, 146-47
Clinic
  diagnostic, 12
  referral to a, 184
Clothes
  child ripping off his, 106
  girl's interest in, 100
  loose, for boys, 101
Communication, 19, 166, 180, 183
Community
  humiliation by the, 38
  rejection of the, 38
  social attitudes of the, 94
Companionship, 66
Compulsion, 106-07
Condoms, 35, 36
Confession, a child's, 114
Constipation, youngster's, 134
Consultation, with psychiatrists, 152
Control
  of child, 19, 30, 105, 170
  of natural functions, 50
  of parents', own irritations, 4, 25
Counseling
  guidance, 33
  services, 184
Cowardliness, child's, 140-41
Crawling, kid's, on the floor, 27
Curiosity, mutual sexual, 32, 36, 38

Daydreaming, 164
Deafness, 59, 65
Defectiveness, 15
Deformities, 59
Delinquency, 119

Deprivation, used to enforce authority, 114-15
Deviation, in sex play, 30, 38
Disability (child's), 59
Disfigurement, child with, 63
Dishonesty, 75
Disrespect (child's), 39, 110
Distrust, for boys, 34
Doctor, playing, 159-60
Dog, smelling the behind of, 55-56
Dream world (child's), 144
Drooling, 23
Drugs
  addiction, 182
  for hyperactive kids, 182
Dumbness, 65

Earaches, 62
Earthquake, effect on children, 140
Education, emphasis placed on, 117
  sexual, 36
Embarrassment, 27
Emotional
  conflict, 62
  disturbance, severe, 124
Emotionality (youngsters'), 47
Emotions, blocking out sexual, 101
Endurance, 43
Enema(s), 55
Energy
  outlet for pent-up nervous, 21
  rechanneling of kid's, 27, 48
Environment, child's testing his mastery of the, 172
Epilepsy (child's), 63-64
Erections, 101, 152-53
Erotic games, 30
Eroticism, 23, 29
Exhibitionism, 35, 36
Expectations, unrealistic, 178
Eyelash-picking, 135-36
Eyesight, 59

Family
  adjusting to the ground rules of the, 176
  child intimidating a whole, 43
  disaster, beginning of, 40
  influence of handicapped child on, 60

# INDEX

Family *(Continued)*
   service agency, 184
   stability of the family, undermined, 172
Fantasies
   acting out of, 151
   considered taboo, 151
   incestual, 32
   sexual, 102
Fear(s)
   of germs, 146
   of ghosts, 144
   of growing up, 143
   overcoming, 40, 42, 145
   reasonable, 139
   unreasonable, 139
Feelings, overinvolvement with child's, 181
Feet-stamping, 132
Femininity, 98
   dissatisfaction with, 100
   uncertainty of, 100
Fidgetiness, 135, 136
Fingernail-biting, 21
Fist-banging, 136
Fit(s), child's, 41
Forgiveness, 109, 114, 132
Frustration (child's), 39
   ability to endure, 43
   coming out as protest and rebellion, 172
   relative inability to cope with, 106
   sensitivity to respond to, 41
Fury, child's, 39, 44

Games
   sexual content in physical contact, 33
   wrestling between girls, 33
Genitals, 31
   drawings of dirty doodles of, 126
   hair-pulling on, 21
   snapshots of kid's, 34
Germs, phobia of, 40, 42, 145, 146
Ghosts, 144
Goals, impossible, 176-77
Graffiti, 110
Gratification, devious, in sex, 38
Gutter words, 22-23, 50

Habits, of children
   annoying, 19, 20
   bed-wetting, 26
   changing, 21
   hair-pulling, 21
   messy, 23
   nail-biting, 21
   nose-picking, 19-28
   parents breaking kid's, 19, 26
   provocative, 20
   spending, 134
   TV-viewing, inability to control, 170-71
Hair-pulling, on chest and genitals, 21, 31
Handicap, 11
Harelip, 63
Hemophilia, 68
Hearing, hard of, 59
Heterosexuality, 30, 33
Hitting, 25-26
Homosexuality, 30, 34, 102, 153
Hospitalization, temporary, 12
Humiliation
   avoidance of child's, 20
   by the community, 38
   of parents by child's cheating, 72
Hunchback, 66
Hyperactivity, 47, 182
Hyperthyroidism, 175
Hypoglycemia, 175

Image, nude, 101
Imagination, child's, 144, 171
Immodesty, 152
Immunity, to noise, 133
Inadequacy
   parents' feelings of, 16
   physical, 59
Incentive, to help the kid, 25
Incest, 29-30
   fantasies, 32
Incestual desires, acting out, 155
Indecisiveness, 130
Independence, child's, 168, 173
Influence, on child's behavior, 16, 34
Ingratitude, 178
Inhibition(s), 29, 154
Instinct(s), 29
   mastering of, 62

## INDEX

Institution(s), credibility of, 9
Intellect, child's, 117-27
Intellectual potential, child's, 117-18, 119
Intelligence, child's, 124
Intercourse, 33, 35
Intimacies, exchange of, in sex play, 31
Intimidation, 43
Intolerance, 40
Irritation, parents controlling their, 25
Isolation, of child, 44
"Itching," 136

Jealousy, 42, 154

Knives, playing with, 86

Learning capacity, child's, 118
Lesbian tendencies, 97, 103
License, parental, 37, 114
Licking, 21-2
Lip-picking, 21
Loneliness, 163
Lopsidedness, 124
Lotto, 172
Love
  capacity to, 29
  child's uncertainty of parents', 42
Lying, 69-80

Manicure, 21
Manners, bad, 72
Masturbation, 32, 94-95, 101
  as a pacifier, 96
Matches, playing with, 86
Maturity, consciousness of, 35
Medical attention, for child, 175
Messiness, 50
Messy habits, 23
Mind, child's
  extraordinary keen, 124
  one-track, 40
Misbehavior, child's, 41, 51, 57, 58
Mischievousness, 114
"Molesting," 33

Mongoloids, 64
Morality, 35
Motivation, 10
Mutilation, 21

Nail-biting, 21
Nakedness, 32, 155
Natural functions, sensitivity about, 50
Nervous system, child's, 105
Noise, immunity to, 133
Nose-picking, child's
  advice to parents in case of, 20
  in class, 20
Nude images, kids staring at their, 101
Nudity, 154, 155

"Oddball," sexual, 93
Over-aggressiveness, child's, 48
Over-discipline, 115
Overinvolvement, with child's feelings, 181
Over-protection, of the kid, 115

Panties, sniffing, 30
Pants-wetting, 26-27
Parental authority, 173
Parenthood, 37, 40, 178
Parents
  and control of their kids, 19, 30
  attitude to destructive child, 105-06
  attitude to homosexual child, 102
  attitudes about sex, 29
  authority, 17, 37, 114
  breaking kid's habits, 26
  calmness, 39
  chastisement by, 46
  child as source of shame to, 19
  communication between themselves, 19
  consolation for child, 45-46
  constitutional limitations on, 176, 177-78
  controlling their irritation, 25
  -child relationships, 9, 11, 25, 26, 31, 34, 35

Parents *(Continued)*
　criticism from, 19
　dealing with kid's pants-wetting, 27
　detection of kid's sexual behavior, 30
　developing closeness to child, 46
　drastic actions by, 38
　feelings of inadequacy, 16
　handling child's self-mutilation, 21
　handling reaction against child's blasphemy, 25
　incentive in a shy way, 25
　keeping up their self-esteem, 40
　passionate feelings of, 39
　patience, for kid's misbehavior, 47
　permissive, 151
　protecting child from hurting, 42
　punishment by, 37
　reaction to kid's bed-wetting, 26-27
　reaction to kid's good behavior, 42
　reaction to kid's rages, 41
　reaction to kid's using gutter words, 23
　rechanneling of child's aggressiveness, 48
　responsibility of, 10
　restrictive measures of, 38
　self-control, 4
　self-sacrificing, 17
　sense of humor, 178
　sense of power, 178
　sense of proportion, 19, 41
　sense of wonder, 179
　shy, 151
　tensions, 16
　upset by some sex plays, 30
　use of good sense by, 40
　using deprivation to enforce authority, 114
Penis, 31, 101, 126
Perfectionist, "cure" of a, 40
Permissiveness, 151
Personality, regard for child's, 35, 177
Perversity, 122, 155
Physical handicap, child's, 175
Physical hangups, 59-68
Pills, birth control, 35

Pimples, 61
Playacting, 137
Pornography, 29
Pot smoking, 84
Pregnancy, out of wedlock, 35-36
Privacy
　need of, 32
　self-imposed, 164
Professional counsel, 184
Professional guidance, 176
Professional help, 13, 15-16
Professional treatment, 183
Progressiveness, sexual, 30
Promiscuity, 36
　dangers of, 102
Protection, 115
Protest, against frustration, 172
Provocation, child's, 20, 39
Psychiatrists, 12, 138
Psychoanalysis, 140
Psychologists, 12
Psychotherapy, 111, 182, 183
Psychotic, child, 54
Pubic hair, comparing of, 31
Punishment, 37

Rages, frequent, 41
Rambunctiousness, child's, 47-48
Realism, 178
Reassurance, need for, 134
Rebellion, against frustration, 72
Recklessness, child's, 47-48
Reeducation, child's, 7, 40, 179
　emotional, 118
Rehabilitation, of youngsters, 7, 11
Rejection, of the community, 38
Repatterning, in masculine form, behavior, 100
Residential care for children, 15
Residential treatment centers, 12, 183, 184
Retardation, 15, 118
Retraining, of child, 7
Risk, in using parental license, 37

Sedatives, 132
Seduction, 34, 35, 37, 158
Seductive gestures, 154, 158
Self-confidence, 140

# INDEX

Self-control, 105
Self-defense, 141
Self-discipline, values of, 17, 179
Self-doubt, 130
Self-esteem
  build up in child, 65
  parents', 40
Self-mutilation, child's
  by biting his toenails, 21
  by pulling his hair, 21
  by picking his lips, 21
Sense of humor, 178
Sense of independence, 168, 173
Sense of power, 178
Sense of proportion, 19, 141
Sense of shame, about natural functions, 49-58
Sense of wonder, 179
Sensitivity (in youngsters), 16-17, 48, 167
  about natural functions, 50
  delicate, 132
  to respond to frustration, 41
  to tics and fidgets, 129
Service(s)
  counseling, 184
  family, agency, 184
  residential, 12, 15, 183, 184
Sex
  devious gratification in, 38
  differences, blurring of, 29
  frankness about, 29
  hangups, 29
  in pornography, 29
  "oddball" behavior, 94
  parents' attitude about, 29
Sex games with adults, 151-61
Sex play
  deviation in sex play, 30, 38
  exchange of intimacies in, 31
  indulging in, 29
  parents upset by, 30
Sexiness, 100, 101
Sexual
  behavior, 30
  content in physical-contact games, 33
  curiosity, mutual, 32, 36, 38
  deviation, 30, 38
  education, 36
  emotions, 101

fantasy, 102, 151
identification, difficulty of, 100
intimate expression, 33
maturity, 94
"oddball," 93
peculiarities, 93-104
progressiveness, 30
relationship, mutual consent in, 101
standards, 153
stimulation, 33, 101
Shame, 49-58
  child as source of, to parents, 19
  sense of, about natural functions, 49
"Shock treatments," 136
Shyness, 139, 151, 163, 168-69
Siblings, jealousy of, 42
Slobbering, 23-24
Social
  attitudes of the community, 94
  isolates, 164
  maturity, 94
  ostracism, 27
Soiling, child's, 49
Sophistication, child's, 117
Speech defect, 23
Spending habits, 134
Squirming, 132
Stack-blowing, 39-48
Standards, sexual, 153
Stealing, 49, 69, 80
Stimulation, sexual, 33, 101
Stupidity, 122
Submission, 111
  drugging a child into, 182
Superparent, 182
Supersensitivity, 132
Superstition, 148

Tantrum(s), 39, 40, 42
  removing irritants of, 44
Temper, child's, 39, 43, 46, 108
Therapy, behavioral conditioning, 136
Tics and fidgets, 129-38
"Tightness," 134
Toilet
  paper, writing notes on, 52
  relishing the smell of a, 56
  training, 50-51

Tolerance, 65, 111, 136
   raising the level of, 178
Trauma, child's, 139-40
TV viewing habits, inability to control, 176

"Ugly ducklings," 59
Unisex clothes, 34
Uniqueness, in child, 48
Unpredictability of kids, 40
Upbringing, child's, 39
Urinating, 53, 99, 100
Urological problem, boy's, 101

Vagina, 51
   biological functions of the, 126
   poking objects up the, 52
Venereal disease, dangers of, 35, 102
Violence, show of potential, 39, 44
Vomiting, 133
Vulgarity, 96-97

Wishful thinking, 172
Withdrawal, 163-64
Womanhood, 33
Women's lib, 34
Wrestling matches, between girls, 33